THE ULTIMATE MIXED MARTIAL ARTIST

THE FIGHTER'S MANUAL TO STRIKING COMBINATIONS, TAKEDOWNS, THE CLINCH, AND CAGE TACTICS

Anderson Silva
Forrest Griffin
Randy Couture
Jon Fitch
Karo Parisyan
Greg Jackson
Shawn Tompkins
Anuwat Kaewsamrit
Dave Camarillo
Erin Toughill
Shawn Yarborough

New York Times Bestselling Author
ERICH KRAUSS

LAS VEGAS

First Published in 2009 by Victory Belt Publishing.

ISBN 10: 0-9815044-7-7

ISBN 13: 978-0-9815044-7-6

This book is for educational purposes. The publisher and authors of this instructional book are not responsible in any manner whatsoever for any adverse effects arising directly or indirectly as a result of the information provided in this book. If not practiced safely and with caution, martial arts can be dangerous to you and to others. It is important to consult with a professional martial arts instructor before beginning training. It is also very important to consult with a physician prior to training due to the intense and strenuous nature of the techniques in this book.

Victory Belt ® is a registered trademark of Victory Belt Publishing.

Cover Design by Michael J. Morales, VIP GEAR

Printed in Hong Kong

Contents

PART ONE: STRIKING

BASIC STRIKES

PUNCHES

KICKS

ELBOW STRIKES

KNEE STRIKES

DEFENDING AGAINST STRIKES

DEFENDING AGAINST PUNCHES

DEFENDING AGAINST KICKS

DEFENDING AGAINST KNEES

ATTACKING COMBINATIONS

PUNCHING COMBINATIONS

PUNCH / KICK COMBINATIONS

PART TWO: STRIKING TO THE TAKEDOWN AND TAKEDOWN DEFENSE

STRIKING TO THE TAKEDOWN

TAKEDOWN DEFENSE

PART THREE: THE CLINCH

THE DIRTY BOXING CLINCH

THE MUAY THAI CLINCH

OVER-UNDER CLINCH / HEAD AND ARM CLINCH

DOUBLE UNDERHOOK CLINCH

BACK CONTROL CLINCH

OPPONENT PRESSED AGAINST CAGE

OPPONENT PRESSING YOU AGAINST CAGE

Introduction

In this book some of the world's best mixed martial artists come together to share their most effective techniques and strategy concerning the stand-up element of the MMA fight game. They cover basic strikes, striking defense, attacking combinations, counterattacking combinations, striking to the takedown, takedown defense, the dirty boxing clinch, the Muay Thai clinch, the neutral clinches, the double underhook clinch, the back control clinch, and even various techniques for turning the cage into a strategic weapon. While every fighter has a different take on what is most effective in MMA, each of the techniques in this book have been utilized effectively at the highest levels of competition, proving that no one style can be deemed "the best." Unlike most MMA instructional books, this manual does not provide just one point of view. It provides many, and to get the most out of it, you must decide what works best for you. In addition to drilling the various techniques presented, it is also important to develop your personal strategy, as well as your footwork, timing, speed, and power through drills and exercises. Below is a brief list of some of the things world-renowned MMA fight coach Shawn Tompkins suggests to include into your daily training regimen and fight preparation:

STRATEGY

When preparing for a fight you should always look at your opponent's last three or four fights. With fighters constantly evolving, going back farther than that is oftentimes pointless because he will most likely have corrected a lot of his weaknesses and developed new strengths. While watching the tapes, you want to look at your opponent's habits. If you notice that every time he gets hit with a cross he resorts to street-fighting mode and retaliates with a cross of his own, you want to employ combinations that turn your body away from his power hand. If you notice that he clearly outclasses you in the striking department, then you want to utilize combinations that allow you to crowd your opponent and execute a takedown. If you see that he has an exceptional ground game but is limited with striking on his feet, you want to employ striking combinations that don't make you vulnerable to the takedown. The goal is to glean everything you can about your opponent through his fight tapes, make a list of his strengths, his weaknesses, and his reactions, and then tailor your game plan and training to capitalize on these aspects. In this book, you will learn how some of the best fighters and coaches in the business accomplish certain goals. Learning as many of these variations as possible will make your style more flexible, and flexibility will dramatically help you to tailor your game plan for a specific opponent.

SPARRING

Sparring is one of the most important things that you can do to prepare for an upcoming fight. Hitting the mitts and heavy bag does wonders to improve technique, but sparring is where you develop a realistic sense of timing and distance. Most fighters make the largest gains when sparring three times a week. Instead of going to war with your training partners, go at 70 percent speed two times a week. Having already developed a specific game plan for your upcoming fight, work on maintaining that game plan even while getting hit. During the third session of sparring, go full speed to keep yourself honest. However, it is important not to go full speed every time you spar. There are fighters and fighting gyms that harness this war mentality, believing that it creates toughness. While this is often true, taking hard blows to the head on a daily basis can hurt you severely down the road. Every time you take a hard shot to the face or head, your brain collides with your skull, creating scar tissue around your brain. The more scar tissue you have, the easier you are to knock out. If you doubt this, look at many of the legends of the sport. Many of the fighters who had iron jaws when first starting out are now getting knocked out with strikes that they would have once brushed off with a smile. A lot of this has to do with too much hard sparring.

In addition to monitoring the speed at which you spar, it is also very important to pick and choose your sparring partners. If you are fighting an excellent wrestler with limited striking skills, you don't want to be sparring with professional kickboxers. Along this same line, if your upcoming opponent is a southpaw, there is no point sparring with orthodox fighters because it is a completely different game. If there aren't any southpaws in your gym to train with, you must go on the road to find some. You don't have to move to a new city and sign up at a new gym, but you should spend at least a few weeks sparring with partners that fight in a similar fashion as your upcoming opponent.

PAD WORK

As already mentioned, you should tailor your game plan to capitalize on your opponent's weaknesses. A part of this is developing striking combinations based on your opponent's most common reaction to strikes. For example, if your opponent drops his arms every time he gets hit with a body shot, you will want to train combinations that include a strike to the body followed by a strike to the head. Hitting the focus mitts or Thai pads is a way to ingrain these combinations into your subconscious. If you're facing a fighter who likes to pressure his opponents, have your trainer pressure you with the Thai pads as you unleash your combinations. If your opponent likes to remain on the outside, have your trainer constantly move away from you as you advance with your strikes. In addition to helping you build specific combinations, pad work is also almost as effective as sparring when it comes to developing your timing, sense of distance, and accuracy. Unlike when doing bag work, you are striking at a live, moving body. As you run through your combinations, have your trainer correct your form and dial in the details. If you are not confident in his ability to do this, videotape your pad work sessions, watch them

immediately after training, and then write notes on what you are doing wrong.

HEAVY BAG WORK

Although there are speed drills that you can do on the heavy bag, your main intent is to develop your power. Instead of tapping your target as you sometimes do when training on the focus mitts, you want to drill your kicks and punches into the heavy leather. Where a lot of fighters go wrong with bag work is they stand stationary in front of it, throwing one strike after the next. Unless you are planning to fight your upcoming opponent in a similar fashion, this will not help you develop your skills. Every time you hit the heavy bag, it moves, just like an opponent. To get the most out of this training, follow the heavy bag from side to side and front to back. Move in and out of range. For the best results, it is also important to have your coach watch you as you train. While conducting pad or mitt work, it is often difficult for him to monitor your stance and form as you strike because he is the one holding the pads. When you are working on the heavy bag, he can see all parts of your body clearly and correct anything you may be doing wrong. The other nice part about bag work is that it is an exercise that you can do when your coach or training partners are not available. When working solo, it is important to video tape your training sessions. Video never lies, and it is an excellent way to keep you honest. In addition to helping you discover what you are doing wrong, videotaping your heavy bag sessions also tend to keep you from getting lazy. Knowing that you will be watching the footage later, you throw all your punches and kicks with intent to do damage.

SHADOW BOXING

Shadow boxing helps develop your footwork. Where a lot of fighters go wrong with shadow boxing is they throw lazy strikes and stand in one location. They treat it as a warm-up rather than a drill to improve their fighting skills. Anytime you step into the gym, you should have a specific goal in mind. If your goal is to improve on certain combinations, practice those combos while shadow boxing. You must visualize your opponent. If you throw a jab, lash it straight out between your imaginary opponent's arms. Visualize his reaction to that jab, and then move in such a way that you can capitalize upon that reaction. A helpful tool is to place a medicine ball on the mats and then shadow box around it. Always be mindful of your stance. When your stance changes by just three inches, it dramatically changes your offense and defense. It affects the types of punches you can throw, as well as how hard you can throw. Again, it can be very beneficial to have your coach watch your shadow boxing sessions. If you are repeatedly making the same mistake, have him tailor your mitt and pad work to correct that mistake. Just as with heavy bag work, shadow boxing is something that you can do when your coach or training partners aren't available. You can do it in your garage or living room. Again, when performing shadow boxing drills by yourself, it is in your best interest to videotape your sessions to see where you need to improve.

ISOLATION DRILLS

There are countless drills that you can do to improve your fighting skills, but it is important to do drills that are going to help you with your upcoming fight. While it can be beneficial to hone in on and develop certain aspects of your game by doing two man boxing drills, two man kickboxing drills, and two man wrestling drills, it is also important to choose drills that prepare you for your specific opponent. For example, if you are going to fight a superior striker and want to take the fight to the mat, you don't want to practice takedowns on a wrestler because he utilizes a different stance and different takedown defenses than your upcoming opponent. A better game plan would be to practice a drill called "Big Glove/Little Glove." To perform it, your opponent puts on sixteen ounce gloves and you wear MMA gloves. Your opponent's job is to throw hard punches to your body and head, and your job is to avoid those punches and score a takedown. Once you control your opponent on the mat, you return to the standing position.

Another excellent option is to perform a three-man wrestling drill. Start in the middle of the ring or cage and have three of your training partners surround you. When the buzzer sounds, begin taking them down one after another using various techniques. For the first minute, your opponents will defend using 65 percent of their max effort. For the second minute, they will use 75 percent of their max effort. By the fifth minute, when you are utterly exhausted, they are defending your takedowns using 100 percent of their max effort. Although it will be often be nearly impossible to complete a successful takedown with no energy and your opponents fighting you with all their energy, it makes you mentally stronger and a better wrestler. It also mimics what might happen during a real fight. The worst time to wrestle your opponent is when you are exhausted, but if you have already suffered through that time and again in training, it allows you to pull through and not give up in an actual fight.

If you're fighting an excellent boxer and have decided your best strategy is to counter his punches with kicks, an excellent drill to include in your daily regimen is "Puncher vs. Kicker," where you assume the roll of the kicker. While sparring, your opponent can only throw punches, and you can only throw kicks. Although you will want to set up your kicks with punches in your actual fight, focusing exclusively on your kicks in training allows you to develop timing, sense of distance, and reaction speed to your opponent's punches. If you have watched your opponent's fight tapes and learned that he wins most of his fights by pressing his opponents up against the cage, an excellent option is to incorporate into your routine a clinch drill where your opponent's only job is to keep you pinned against the fence and your only goal is to escape. If you learn that your opponent often overextends on his punches and you feel your best game plan is to employ a counterattacking strategy, then you might want to incorporate an offensive/defensive striking drill where all you do is slip, parry, and counter your training partner's combinations. No matter what drills you choose to practice, the important part is that they are fight specific. If you are going up against a fighter who has never wrestled a day in his life, you don't want to be conducting drills that focus on takedown defense.

The Contributors

Anderson Silva is the UFC middleweight champion and one of the most feared strikers in the game. Armed with flawless boxing skills, ruthless Muay Thai kicks, knees, and elbows, a devastating clinch, and a ruthless ground game, he is one of the most well-rounded fighters competing in MMA. Silva is the author of *The Mixed Martial Arts Instruction Manual: Striking*, and he is ranked by the vast majority of MMA sites as the number one best pound-for-pound mixed martial artist in the world.

Forrest Griffin was a contestant on the first season of the *The Ultimate Fighter* reality show on Spike TV. In the show's finale, he defeated Stephan Bonnar by unanimous decision, earning him a multifight contract with the UFC. He went on to defeat a number of top light-heavyweight contenders, including Mauricio "Shogun" Rua, and in July 2008, he defeated Quinton Jackson by unanimous decision, earning him the UFC light heavyweight title. Griffin is the New York Times best-selling author of *Got Fight? The Fifty Zen Principles of Hand-to-Face Combat*. He lives in Las Vegas, Nevada.

Randy Couture is a former three-time UFC heavyweight champion and a former two-time UFC light heavyweight champion. He is a UFC Hall of Famer and the only UFC combatant to have held championship belts in two different weight divisions. In addition to his accomplishments in mixed martial arts, Couture is a world-renowned Greco-Roman wrestler and coach. He is the author of **Wrestling for Fighting: The Natural Way** and lives in Las Vegas, Nevada.

Jon Fitch is one of the top-ranked welterweight MMA fighters in the world. Except for his title shot loss to Georges St. Pierre, he is undefeated in the UFC, having earned victories over dangerous fighters such as Diego Sanchez, Thiago Alves, and Josh Burkman. He is a black belt in guerilla jiu-jitsu under Dave Camarillo and trains out of the American Kickboxing Academy in San Jose, California.

Karo Parisyan is a five-time national judo champion and one of the most exciting UFC welterweight competitors. He is known for his dominating clinch game and massive judo throws. He is the author of **Judo For Mixed Martial Arts** and lives in Los Angeles, California.

Greg Jackson is the world's most accomplished MMA trainer. He has more than fifteen MMA champions in his stable, including Georges St. Pierre and Rashad Evans, and his athletes have won hundreds of grappling championships. He is the author of *Jackson's Mixed Martial Arts: The Stand-Up Game* and *Jackson's Mixed Martial Arts: The Ground Game*.

Shawn Tompkins is the head instructor at Xtreme Couture, and he coaches notable fighters such as Randy Couture, Dan Henderson, Sam Stout, Chris Horodecki, Vitor Belfort, Wanderlei Silva, Kimbo Slice, and Jay Hieron. He is a Bas Rutten MMA Systems representative, owner and creator of Team Tompkins Fighting Systems, and a third-degree black belt in Shotokan karate.

Anuwat Kaewsamrit, a professional Muay Thai kickboxer, is a former Lumpini and four-time Rajadamnern Stadium champion. He has eighty-five career wins, with thirty-seven of those wins coming by way of knockout. Known for his devastating punches, he his often referred to as "The Iron Hands of Siam." He fights and coaches out of Kaewsamrit Gym in Bangkok, Thailand.

Dave Camarillo is a world-renowned black belt in both judo and Brazilian jiu-jitsu. He is the head jiu-jitsu coach at the American Kickboxing Academy and trains notable fighters such as Jon Fitch, Mike Swick, Josh Koscheck, and Cain Velasquez. He is the author of *Guerrilla Jiu-Jitsu: Revolutionizing Brazilian Jiu-Jitsu*.

Erin Toughill is one of the original pioneers of women's MMA, and she is the only woman to ever be simultaneously ranked in the "top five" of both MMA and professional boxing. She has competed in Japan's biggest MMA tournaments and fought for several championship belts. Most recently, Erin played the roll of "Steel" on NBC's popular remake of *American Gladiators*.

Shawn Yarborough has been competing in Muay Thai for fourteen years. He has won numerous titles in the International Kickboxing Federation and the World Kickboxing Association. Yarborough was the silver medalist in the IKA World Championships in Italy in 2002, and he won the King's Cup Gold Medal in Thailand in 2006. He is the Muay Thai coach at the Warrior Training Center in Las Vegas, and trains MMA fighters such as Forrest Griffin, Gina Carano, Wanderlei Silva, Jay Hieron, Brandon Vera, and Mike Pyle.

PUNCHES
(p. 24-30)

This section gives step-by-step instructions on how to execute the punches most commonly utilized in MMA competition. While you might already be familiar with several of these punches from other martial arts such as boxing or Muay Thai, it is important to pay close attention to the details because the dynamics of punches often change when applied to MMA. For example, boxers will sometimes put a lot of weight on their front knee while throwing a jab. Although this can work well in a boxing match, it can make you vulnerable to a takedown in MMA. These small adjustments are important to adopt because they will help you flow from one strike to another without putting yourself in unnecessary danger.

As you will notice in this section, it is also very important to utilize your entire body rather than just your upper body when throwing punches. When you employ your shoulders, hips, and legs, you not only conserve energy with your punches, but you also generate a lot more power. To ensure your progress while practicing your basic punches, watch yourself in the mirror and routinely ask yourself, "Am I stepping right, rolling my shoulders, and properly utilizing my reach?" Constantly correcting your mistakes will prevent you from developing bad habits down the road.

KICKS
(p. 31-37)

There are only a handful of fighters competing in the top tier of MMA who don't utilize kicks. Although kicks can make you vulnerable because they force you to balance on one leg, which decreases your stability, they are an extremely versatile tool that can achieve a number of different goals. The tricky part is finding the right kick for the job. For example, when up against a good boxer, throwing low round kicks to his lead leg can quickly sap power from his punches. The more you damage his legs, the more difficult it will be for him to throw intricate punching combinations. If you are up against a good counterstriker, concluding your combinations with a front kick or round kick is an excellent way to knock him off balance and make it difficult for him to launch a speedy retaliation.

There are kicks that can exploit the weaknesses of just about every type of fighter, but due to the fact that you are lifting one foot off the mat, they should almost always be set up utilizing other strikes. In addition to making it more difficult for your opponent to catch your kicks, defend against them, or even counter with a strike of his own such as a right cross, setting up your kicks will also make them more effective. For example, if you want to deliver a hard rear round kick to your opponent's ribs, setting it up with a lead hook is an excellent option because your punch not only pulls your opponent's focus away from his legs, but it also pushes his body into the kick, making it more powerful.

While practicing kicks in the gym, in addition to working on developing your power and speed, it is also extremely important to work on your accuracy. A novice kicker will simply lash his leg out without much care for placement, and while he will often cause his opponent damage, he will just as often cause himself damage by kicking elbows and knee caps. An advanced kicker can place his kick within centimeters of his target every time, allowing him to repeatedly strike the same spot on his opponent's leg or drive his shin into his opponent's liver or kidney. The key to being successful with kicks is not rushing them. Before throwing one, scope out your opponent's weaknesses, pick your exact target, and most importantly set your kick up.

some are best thrown vertically, others cause more damage when thrown horizontally into your opponent's body.

ELBOWS STRIKES
(p. 37-40)

Elbows are designed for opening cuts on your opponent's face, making them one of the most dangerous strikes in the sport of MMA. For illustration purposes, this section demonstrates the six primary elbow strikes from punching range. However, it is important to note that the majority of these strikes can also be used when tied up in the clinch, when you have your opponent pressed up against the cage, when breaking away from a tie-up position, or on the ground. When studying the techniques, the one thing to pay special attention to is the rotation of your hips. With the elbow strike being a short weapon, it is very difficult to generate a significant amount of power with your shoulder alone. To cause damage, you must employ your entire body.

KNEES
(p. 41-42)

In the past few years, knee strikes have become a much more popular of a weapon in mixed martial arts, primarily due to the number of wrestlers competing in the sport. When you are up against a phenomenal wrestler, throwing kicks can be a dangerous venture. With the majority of kicks traveling along a circular path, wrestlers will often catch your kick to their advantage. Sometimes they will snatch your kicking leg and then sweep your grounded leg out from underneath you, and other times they will avoid your kick altogether by shooting straight into your body for the takedown. In either case, you fail to cause your opponent damage and he achieves his goal of putting you on your back.

Knee strikes are a lot less risky to throw when up against a wrestler with excellent takedowns. Not only are they harder for him to catch, but they also travel linearly. If you're up against a wrestler and he knows you have dangerous knees, he will be a lot more hesitant to shoot in for takedown for fear of eating a knee strike to the face.

In addition to being an excellent form of takedown defense, knee strikes are also a great weapon when tied up in the clinch or when you end up in close range after a striking combination. The one thing you should pay close attention to when studying the strikes in this section is the trajectory of your knees. While

DEFENDING PUNCHES
(p. 43-47)

Learning how to defend against punches not only helps you to avoid taking abuse, but it also helps create openings to attack. When your opponent is in his fighting stance, he has full mobility. If you throw a strike, he can use his defensive lines to block it or simply move out of the way. However, when your opponent throws a punch and you make him miss, his balance is momentarily shattered and his defenses are down. As long as you utilize proper form while evading, you will be left in a good position to capitalize on your opponent's weakness with strikes of your own or a takedown. To help develop the skills demonstrated in this section, I strongly recommend engaging in a type of sparring drill where your opponent throws nothing but punches and you have to avoid them using slips and parries. Once you get comfortable with this drill, the next step is to add counters. Your opponent leads the action ever time with punches, you evade his shot and make him miss, and then you use his awkward positioning to put your hands on him. If you practice these types of drills a couple of times a week, you will not only be a lot harder to hit, but you will also have the ability to make your opponent pay every time he throws a strike. The goal in every fight is to break your opponent mentally and physically, and there is no better way to accomplish that than with evasive maneuvers.

DEFENDING KICKS
(p. 49-52)

This section covers how to defend against the primary kicks used in MMA competition. Some of these defenses require you to move into your opponent's kick to prevent it from reaching maximum velocity, others involve evading the kick altogether, and still others involve simply blocking the strike before it can reach its target. With the exception of the evasive tactics, each of your defenses will most likely cause you some damage. Kicks are powerful weapons, and no matter what part of your body that you use to block, it is going to hurt. As already mentioned, the goal in any fight is to cause your opponent more damage than he causes you, which can be accomplished in two ways. First, you want to utilize proper form when defending kicks. When done correctly, the techniques shown in this section might cause you some pain, but they will cause your opponent more pain. Second, you want to immediately launch a counterattack after defending a kick. With your opponent balanced on one leg, you have a golden opportunity to attack with either strikes or a takedown. Many of these retaliatory strikes will be demonstrated in the counterattacks section, but in the beginning it is very important to focus on your form. If your kicking defense is sloppy, you will not have the base or balance to capitalize on your opponent's awkward positioning.

DEFENDING KNEES
(p. 52-53)

As already mentioned, knee strikes are becoming ever more popular in MMA competition, making it an important strike to learn how to block. While it is a lot more difficult to defend against knee strikes than it is kicks and punches, this section offers a few techniques that can come in very handy. Although one focuses on redirecting your opponent's knee to evade his strike and the other focuses on driving your elbow into his knee to cause him damage, they both have the same goal—to disrupt your opponent's base and balance and create an opportunity to launch an attack of your own.

PUNCHING COMBINATIONS
(p. 54-70)

This section covers basic and advanced punching combinations. While it can be more fun to learn advanced five-punch combinations, it is important to take baby steps. When first starting out, focus on perfecting two- and three-punch combinations. Work on your form and your fluidity between strikes. Once you have mastered those, move onto the four- and five-punch combinations. The goal is not to see how fast you can unleash them—the goal is to make your opponent respect each punch in your combination. If you lead with a lazy jab, your opponent will most likely counter before you get to your second punch. Also work on your accuracy. If a combination requires you to go high with a hook and then low with a body shot to keep your opponent guessing, make sure the hook connects with your opponent's chin or behind his ear and the body shot digs into his solar plexus. If either strike is off target, you will fail to distract your opponent and create openings for your follow-up strikes.

It is important to note that although each of the combinations included in this section have been utilized time and again

in MMA, they are not the only combinations out there. Once you have mastered the techniques on the coming pages, it is important to experiment to discover what works best for you. It is also important to build combinations that will exploit your opponent's weaknesses and positioning. For example, if your opponent is overly aggressive, employing combinations that focus heavily on body shots can do wonders to slow him down.

PUNCH / KICK COMBINATIONS
(p. 71-103)

This section covers a broad array of punch-kick combinations that have proved effective at the top levels of MMA competition. Just as with punches, it is important to walk before you run. When first starting out, focus on the simple combinations where you are using punches to set up a single kick. Where a lot of new students go wrong is they focus so intently on throwing the kick, their punches suffer. And when you fail to threaten your opponent with your punches, he will most likely see the kick coming from a mile away and either get out of the way, block your strike, or counter with a strike of his own.

Once you feel comfortable with the basic combos, move on to the more advanced ones. With these, focus on flowing from one strike into the next to limit your opponent's ability to counter. Remember, the goal is to get one step ahead of your opponent at all times. As he shifts his focus high to defend your punches, switch to kicks, and as he shifts the focus low to deal with your kicks, go back to punches.

With a lot of combinations shown, it is also very important to pay close attention to footwork. As you will see, many of the strikes thrown in the more advanced combinations allow you to acquire a dominant angle of attack, which means you are in a great position to launch your next strike, but your opponent is in a terrible position to either block that strike or counter with a strike of his own.

ELABORATE COMBINATIONS
(p. 104-115)

This section combines the punch, kick, elbow, and knee strikes you learned earlier into intricate combinations. While there are an infinite number of combinations that can be put together utilizing these various tools, the ones demonstrated here will teach you how to move in and out of range to deliver the various strikes. It also unveils what many consider unorthodox techniques, such as spinning backfists and spinning back elbows. While these strikes require you to turn your back to your opponent and can make you vulnerable to takedowns and strikes, they can also lead to high reward. However, it is recommended that you learn the basic combinations before moving onto these more advanced techniques.

your opponent's fist by mere inches, making timing and sense of distance crucial, but when performed correctly, they will leave you in an excellent position to counter. Just as with the jab, the goal is to capitalize on your opponent's awkward positioning and cause as much damage as possible. If you delay, he will pull his outstretched arm back into his stance and either put up his guard or launch another strike.

COUNTERING THE JAB
(p. 116-121)

Learning how to launch a counterattacking combination off your opponent's jab is extremely important because the vast majority of fighters begin their combinations with a jab. If you watched your opponent's fight tapes and know that's generally what he leads with, it is in your best interest to prepare for it. In this section, four effective jab-counterattacking combinations are outlined. With each of them, the goal is to parry your opponent's jab to avoid taking abuse, and then immediately counter with your own combination before he can reestablish his guard and fire off his second strike. This is often harder than it seems, especially when up against an opponent with quick hands. To improve your timing, it is suggested to practice a drill where your opponent throws nothing but jabs, and you counter and immediately launch your attack.

COUNTERING THE CROSS
(p. 122-124)

When you parry or slip your opponent's jab, unless he really overextended on his punch, he will usually still have fairly good base and balance, which means he could easily follow up with another strike. When you slip or evade your opponent's cross, due to the nature of the punch, it will usually momentarily shatter his base and balance, giving you more opportunity to launch a counterattack. However, there is a trade-off. The cross is an extremely powerful punch, and if you fail to properly evade it, there is a good chance that you will go to sleep. As a result, you must make a split-second decision when a cross comes at you. If you don't have the proper footing, it is most likely in your best interest to simply back away from it. Although this takes you out of the fight and limits your ability to counter, it is better than taking a shot on the chin. If you feel you have the proper footing and timing, then it is often in your best interest to evade the shot using the lean-back or a slip. Both techniques require you to evade

COUNTERING THE HOOK
(p. 126-129)

This section offers the primary methods for evading your opponent's hooks, which in turn allow you to use his compromised positioning to launch a counterattack. As with most defensive techniques, evasion is better than blocking because you avoid taking any abuse and disrupt your opponent's balance by causing him to miss. However, it is important to be very mindful of the type of opponent you are up against. Because the hook is a circular strike, it is not possible to parry or slip it. Your only two options are to move away from the strike or drop beneath it. If you choose the latter and your opponent is a versatile striker, it is quite possible that he will lead with a hook to get you to drop your level and then follow up with a knee strike to your face. While this would lead one to believe that blocking the hook with your arm is the preferred technique for this punch, this can also be risky. Unlike in boxing, MMA gloves are extremely small. When you press your arm to the side of your head to block a hook, there are still gaps in your protective shield, which often allow your opponent's fist to collide with the side of your head. If your sole goal is to avoid taking abuse, your best bet is to simply get out of the way, but this isn't always possible and will take you out of the fight. For the best results, vary your reactions to your opponent's hooks to confuse him. For example, fade away from your opponent's first hook to cause him to miss. When he throws another hook, bob and weave underneath it and then capitalize on his awkward positioning by launching a counterattack. By constantly switching up your defense, he will have a very difficult time tailoring his combinations to your reactions.

COUNTERING KICKS
(p. 131-143)

This section demonstrates a number of ways to evade or block your opponent's kicks, and then use his awkward positioning to launch a counterattack of your own. When studying the techniques, it is important to remember that speed is a very important factor. Although the majority of techniques will off-balance your opponent in some fashion, if you delay with your counterattack, he will most likely return to his fighting stance, closing your window of opportunity to score with an easy counter.

COUNTERING KNEES
(p. 145)

This section demonstrates a simple yet effective way for countering an opponent's knee strike. While it is sometimes best to simply back away from a knee strike to avoid taking any damage, this isn't always possible. Two examples are when your opponent backs you into the cage with punches and then concludes his combination with a knee strike or when you drop your level to shoot in for a takedown and he counters by throwing a knee at your face. In both situations, having this block in your arsenal can not only prevent you from taking damage, but also damage your opponent and destroy his base. As he attempts to recover from your painful block, you can go on the offensive, whether that be with strikes or completing your takedown.

PUINCHES

Jab

Although the jab isn't as powerful as a cross or hook, it is a very versatile punch. Being a very quick strike, it is an excellent tool to generate a reaction out of your opponent. If your opponent reacts to your first few jabs in the same way, you can assume that he will react to your next jab in a similar fashion. This allows you to set up a secondary strike based upon that reaction. For example, if every time you throw a jab your opponent elevates his hands and leans back, following up with a cross to the body would be an excellent option. The jab also is an excellent way to disrupt one of your opponent's attacks. If he launches a multi-punch combination, hitting him in the face with a jab in between his strikes disrupts his rhythm, which allows you to begin your own offensive combination. The biggest problem I see with the jab in MMA is that a lot of fighters pivot on their lead foot and rotate their hips when throwing it. Unlike the cross or hook, the jab does not derive its power from your hips—it generates it's power through the forward movement of your body. To help my fighters develop their jab, I teach them to step forward so that the toes of their lead foot are pointed straight at their opponent, lean slightly forward, and throw the punch straight out into their opponent's face. If you plan on throwing a secondary strike such as a cross or hook, that's when you rotate your hips. As far as a target, I recommend striking the chin or forehead. I'm not a big believer on delivering jabs to your opponent's body because it leaves your head open for hooks and overhands.

1 Junie and I are both in an orthodox fighting stance, searching for an opening to attack.

2 Spotting an opening to throw a jab, I step my left foot forward so that my toes are pointing toward Junie, lean my body slightly forward so that my chest is positioned above my left knee, and throw my left fist straight out.

3 I rotate my left fist so that my palm is facing the mat and strike Junie's chin with the knuckles of my index and middle fingers. It is important to mention that instead of rotating my hips, I generated power for my strike using my forward momentum. Notice how I have kept my right hand elevated to protect the side of my face.

Shawn Tompkins

Cross

The cross is a very aggressive punch that packs knockout power. Unlike the jab, it is thrown with your rear hand, which as a rule should be your dominant hand. Although it can be extremely beneficial to be able to fight just as effectively with your left foot forward as you do with your right, if you're right handed, you generally want to stand with your right leg back. As with the jab, the cross can be used both offensively and defensively. Since the cross has a longer distance to travel due to it being thrown with your rear arm, when utilizing it offensively, you generally want to set it up with a quicker punch, such as a jab. With your opponent stunned or temporarily blinded by your first strike, your chances of landing with the cross increase significantly. However, I prefer to use the cross more than the jab as a counter. The dynamics of the jab require you to place your body weight over your lead knee, which dramatically slows the time it takes to sprawl should your opponent follow his strikes with a takedown. When you throw a cross as a counterpunch, your hips are still balanced, which gives you a free range of movement. While I agree that in kickboxing and boxing the jab is the more dominant defensive weapon, I feel the cross is a lot more effective in MMA, as long as you utilize proper form. To throw a proper cross, begin the punch by flattening your lead foot on the mat and pivoting on the ball of your back foot. At the same time, rotate your hips and shoulders. The combinations of these actions provide all the force needed to knock your opponent out. To generate an added snap to your punch, pull your lead shoulder back as your cross heads out of the chamber. If you throw the cross as you would a haymaker, which generates power from just the shoulder and arm, not only will your punch be slow and telegraphed, but it will also lack serious power. It is also important to keep your chest positioned directly above your lead knee throughout the duration of the strike. If you allow your chest to drift forward over your lead knee, you will have too much weight on your lead leg, which slows your reaction time and saps power from your punch.

My opponent and I are both in orthodox fighting stances, searching for an opening to attack.

Spotting an opening to throw a cross, I plant my left foot solidly on the mat and rotate on the ball of my right foot. As that energy rises up, I rotate my hips and shoulders in a counterclockwise direction and extend my right arm toward my target.

Continuing with my counterclockwise rotation, I turn my fist over so my palm is facing the mat and strike Junie's chin with the knuckles of my index and middle fingers. To protect myself from counterstrikes, I have shrugged my right shoulder above my jaw and kept my left arm elevated. It is important to mention that unlike with the jab, my weight is distributed evenly on both legs.

Shawn Tompkins

Hook

In this sequence I demonstrate how to throw a lead hook. If you look at the second photo, you'll notice that prior to throwing the hook I rotate my body in the opposite direction and come up onto the ball of my back foot, almost as if I am about to throw the cross. This has several benefits. First, it spring-loads your hips and generates more power in your punch. Second, it moves your face away from your centerline, which makes it more difficult for your opponent to hit you with straight punches. Third, it tricks your opponent into believing that you are about to throw a cross. With the cross being a linear punch, your opponent will usually tighten his guard to protect his centerline. However, this leaves the sides of his head and body vulnerable to the hook, which is a circular attack. Just like the cross, the hook generates power from the floor up, but it does so with different dynamics. Once you've made your initial pivot to the outside, plant your rear foot on the mat and pivot on your lead foot. This is often referred to as "sitting on your punch." A perfect example of how sitting on your lead hook can be effective is when your opponent overextends with his cross. To avoid the shot, you begin by slipping to the outside. However, instead of leaning forward with the hook, which would most likely put you too close to your opponent, you plant your back foot on the mat, sit on that leg by shifting your weight backward, and then pivot on the ball of your lead foot so you can land your shot to the back of his ear or the side of his jaw. If you pivot on both feet, as many fighters do, you have a lot less accuracy with your punch.

Personally, I also like to keep my thumb up instead of rotating my hand and turning my thumb toward me. While throwing the hook with the thumb down can be useful in boxing, in MMA it increases your chances of injuring your hand or wrist due to the small gloves. Throwing the punch with your thumb up might not produce as great of a snap, but it allows you to employ your biceps and generate an ample amount of power. If you're using the lead hook to set up a kick with your opposite leg or a takedown, power is more important than snap because you want to disrupt your opponent's base and move him toward your power side. Deciding when to use the lead hook can be tricky. As I already mentioned, it is a great counter to your opponent's cross when both of you are in the same fighting stance. If you're in opposite fighting stances, it's a great counter for your opponent's jab. If you want to use a lead hook as an attack rather than a counterattack, I strongly suggest setting it up with another punch first, such as a jab or cross. Even then, it is very important to utilize proper form so as to not expose your face to counterstrikes. Instead of letting your elbow drift away from your body, which makes that side of your face vulnerable, let the rotation of your hips pull your fist directly off your chin. Throwing your hand off to the side before throwing the hook accomplishes nothing good—it telegraphs your punch, eliminates power, and opens you up for strikes.

1 Junie and I are both in orthodox fighting stances, searching for an opening to attack.

2 To set up a lead hook, I pivot on the ball of my rear foot and rotate my hips and shoulders in a counterclockwise direction. It is important to mention that this is the exact same movement you make when executing an outside slip. As a result, a lead hook is an excellent punch to throw after evading your opponent's cross using an outside slip.

3 Having completed my rotation, I plant my rear foot on the mat, shift my weight backward, pivot on the ball of my lead foot, and begin turning my left arm horizontal to the ground.

4 Still pivoting on the ball of my lead foot, I rotate my shoulders in a clockwise direction and strike the side of Junie's jaw or just behind his ear using the knuckles of my index and middle finger. It is important to notice that I've kept my palm facing toward me instead of rotating it toward the mat. This allows me to pack more power in my punch and push Junie's head toward his left side, which in turn sets me up to throw a strike from the right side of my body, such as a right Thai kick or right cross.

Forrest Griffin

Pivot Hook

In this sequence I demonstrate how to use a lead hook to move to the outside of your opponent's body and establish a dominant angle of attack. To accomplish this, you take an outward step with your lead foot and throw a looping left hook at the same time. As the hook lands, you pivot on your lead foot and slide your rear foot circularly along the canvas. Once positioned off to your opponent's side, he must square his hips with your hips before he can launch an effective strike. Before he can accomplish this, you throw a power shot such as a cross or rear round kick. One thing to keep in mind when executing this technique is that it requires you to circle into your opponent's power. If you attempt to circle to the outside of your opponent's body without throwing the hook, there is a good chance he will plug you with a cross or a rear round kick. Leading with a big, slapping hook is what allows this technique to work. The majority of the time your opponent will slip, cover, or move back to avoid it, making it difficult for him to counter with the cross. However, to be on the safe side, I recommend throwing the hook almost as you would a jab because it allows you to protect your chin with your shoulder. While most fighters employ this technique when pinned up against the cage because it allows them to escape a potentially bad spot, I have found that it works just as well when in the center of the ring. For the best results, you want to make sure to wear khaki pants like I am in the sequence below. Although such pants are absolutely terrible to fight in, they make you look like a super badass yuppie.

Lance and I are in orthodox fighting stances, searching for an opening to attack.

I step my left foot forward and to the outside of Lance's rear foot. At the same time, I rotate my hips in a clockwise direction and throw a lead hook toward the side of his jaw. It is important to notice that I have shrugged my left shoulder to protect the left side of my face and kept my right hand up to protect the right side of my face.

As the hook lands, I pivot on my left foot and slide my right foot in a clockwise direction along the mat. Notice how this positions me off to my opponent's side and gives me a dominant angle of attack. From here, I have an excellent opportunity to throw a cross or rear round kick.

Shawn Tompkins

Uppercut

I believe the uppercut is the most dangerous punch in any striking sport, including boxing, kickboxing, and MMA. When thrown properly, your fist rises straight up into your opponent's chin, which causes his head to fling backward and his brain to slosh violently into his skull. As long as your punch packs power, the majority of the time your opponent will drop. He might quickly recover, but that initial drop almost always occurs. It's also a relatively safe punch to throw when on the inside because your opposite hand is up, protecting your face. The most important thing when throwing an uppercut is to utilize proper form. A lot of fighters like to wind up the punch like Popeye, but that only telegraphs your strike and makes you vulnerable to counterattacks. Instead, begin by rotating your body in the opposite direction of the punch. This motion not only allows you to spring-load your hips, but also it will often make your opponent think that you're throwing a lead hook, causing him to move his arms away from his center to protect the sides of his head. Once accomplished, drop your level and rotate back in the opposite direction. When your hips are square with your opponent, that's when you increase your elevation and bring the punch straight up into his chin. And it's important to not just raise the level of your arm and head—to generate the most power, you want to increase the level of your entire body and stand up into the punch. Unfortunately, the uppercut is not a very versatile strike. Since it requires you to be in close range with your opponent, it is best to set it up with another strike. A lead hook works extremely well because it allows you to close the distance and direct your opponent's hands toward the outside of his face. Also, the movement involved in the lead hook winds your hips in the direction needed to set up the rear uppercut, which eliminates the need to execute the initial body rotation. As a rule of thumb, you don't usually want to throw the uppercut when fighting on the outside. However, later in the book I will demonstrate how to employ it against a wrestler who continuously shoots forward for your rear leg.

Junie and I are both in orthodox fighting stances searching for an opening to attack.

To set up a rear uppercut, I rotate my hips and shoulders in a clockwise direction, just as I would when slipping my opponent's jab.

Having spring-loaded my hips, I drop my level, rotate my hips and shoulders in a counterclockwise direction, and slightly drop my right arm. It is important to notice that I have kept my left arm up to protect myself from counterstrikes.

Increasing my elevation, I rotate my hand so that my palm is facing toward me and strike Junie's chin with the knuckles of my index and middle fingers.

Shawn Tompkins

Overhand

While the overhand isn't utilized that much in boxing, it is a very effective weapon in MMA due to the small gloves worn by the combatants. Land one solid overhand on your opponent's chin and he will most likely drop. The key to being effective with the overhand is acquiring a long base. If your right hand is in the rear, begin by taking an outward step with your left foot. Not only does this step supply you with the range needed to strike your opponent, but it also moves your head away from your centerline, which makes it more difficult for your opponent to hit you with counterstrikes. With your upper body positioned off to the side, float your arm away from your chin and then drive your rear fist circularly toward your opponent's jaw, just as you would when throwing a baseball. The downside to the overhand is that it's a relatively slow strike due to the distance it has to travel, which in turn leaves your face extremely vulnerable. Stepping off to the side certainly reduces that vulnerability, but with your guard momentary dropped, it's still possible to get tagged with a counterstrike. To reduce your susceptibility, it is important to set up the overhand when throwing it as an attack. Personally, I like to lead with a jab to draw my opponent's arms in front of his face, and then come circularly to the side of his head with the overhand. It's an effective attacking combination, but I have found the overhand to be even more effective when used as a counter. If you are in the same fighting stance as your opponent, it's a great counter to his jab. As his fist sails toward your face, step out to the side to evade his shot and then throw the overhand around the outside of his extended arm. With many counterpunches it can be difficult to know if your punch is on target, but not with the overhand. As long as you can connect the crook of your arm with the outside of his elbow, your punch will wrap over his arm and connect with his chin.

Junie and I are in orthodox fighting stances, searching for an opening to attack.

To set up the overhand, I take a small outward step with my left foot. Not only does this prime my hips for a powerful punch, but it also removes my head from Junie's line of fire.

Rotating my hips in a counterclockwise direction, I come up onto the ball of my right foot and throw my fist along an arched path into the side of Junie's jaw. It is important to notice that I've rotated my fist so that I strike with the knuckles of my index and middle fingers.

Shawn Tompkins

Shovel Hook to Body

Body shots can often change the course of a fight. When one of my fighters is up against an extremely aggressive opponent, you'll hear me shout from the corner, "Settle him down! Settle him down!" which means hit him with a right cross to the solar plexus, a left hook to the liver, or a right hook to the kidneys. Landing a cross to the solar plexus takes the wind out of your opponent, and landing a hook to either his liver or kidneys causes that organ to fill up with blood. Not only does that mean less blood for the brain, but it also causes the organ to swell, which prevents the lungs from being able to fully expand. You always know when you've landed a good shot to the liver or kidneys because your opponent's hands will lower, he'll become heavier on his legs, and his overall elevation will drop approximately two inches. It's a great punch to slow an overly aggressive opponent's pace, which in turns allows you to begin your assault. Sometimes it can be beneficial to continually strike the liver or kidneys with body shots, but when I damage either, I like to throw a punch to my opponent's exposed face or throw a kick to his overly stiff legs. The instant he raises his guard or begins checking my kicks, that's when I return to the body shot.

    In the sequence below, I demonstrate how to use a lead left shovel hook to strike your opponent's liver. Just as with many of the punches previously shown, I begin by taking an outward step with my lead foot and rotating my body in the opposite direction of the punch. Again, this removes my head from my centerline, which makes it harder for my opponent to hit my face. It also spring-loads my hips. After I take the step, I'll view my opponent's body and attempt to locate his liver. Once I have the general location in my sights, I'll rotate my body in the opposite direction and throw the shovel hook. It is important to mention that the shovel hook is different than the hook. Instead of my fist approaching the target horizontally, I elevate it diagonally. The goal is to angle your strike so that the shock wave enters into your opponent's liver and then exits his opposite shoulder. The rear shovel hook to the kidneys can be just as effective as the lead shovel hook to the liver, but because the kidneys are located on the backside of the body, you must slightly alter the angle and entry point of your punch.

Junie and I are in orthodox stances, searching for an opening to attack.

To set up the shovel hook to the body, I take an outward step with my left foot and rotate my hips and shoulders in a counterclockwise direction. It is important to mention that this is the same movement I would make when executing an outside slip to evade my opponent's cross.

I drop my left arm slightly and begin rotating my body in a clockwise direction.

Continuing with my clockwise rotation, I drive my fist at a forty-five-degree angle into Junie's liver. The goal is to strike the liver at such an angle that the shock wave travels through his body and out his opposite shoulder.

Shawn Tompkins

Front Kick (rear leg)

You don't see many front kicks in low and mid-level MMA competition, and there is a reason—they make you extremely vulnerable to being taken down, especially when up against an experienced wrestler. However, push kicks can be an extremely valuable tool when utilized at the right moment. One of the best times to employ the push kick is at the end of a combination. When you throw five or six strikes in a row, you usually won't end up in a perfect fighting stance. While you are still off-balance, your opponent will look to retaliate with a combination of his own. By ending your combination with a push kick, you knock your opponent backward, forcing him to reacquire his stance before coming forward. This gives you the time you need to once again return to your proper stance and either launch another combination or prepare to counter your opponent's attack. When you conclude a combination with a push kick, I like to call it "closing the door" because that's essentially what you're doing. You hit your opponent, and then shut the door on him before he can strike back. Gina Carano is an absolute master at this.

A push kick can also be used to set up another kick, such as a switch kick to the liver or a high switch kick. When utilized in this fashion, it's best to target the knee of his lead leg. Not only does this straighten his lead leg, but it also causes his body to lean forward and his hands to drop, creating a pathway for your secondary kick. It is also best to lean slightly back when throwing the push kick because it gives you options—if you want to continue toward your opponent after landing it, you can simply drop your foot down to the mat. However, if your opponent catches your kick or you want to maintain distance, leaning back allows you to quickly pull your leg back toward your body and reacquire your original fighting stance.

Junie and I are in orthodox stances, searching for an opening to attack.

Seeing an opening to land a front kick, I shift my weight onto my lead leg and draw my rear knee toward my chest.

Having elevated my right knee to my chest, I drive the ball of my right foot straight out and into Junie's midsection.

As Junie gets knocked back from my kick, I have two options. I can drop my right foot straight down to the canvas and assume a southpaw stance or I can pull my leg back into my body and reestablish an orthodox stance. The former will keep me in close range, and the latter will create separation.

Shawn Tompkins

Mid Round Kick (rear leg)

The rear round kick to your opponent's midsection is a very powerful strike, but it can also be dangerous to throw. With the kick striking directly underneath your opponent's arm, it's quite easy for him to drop his arm and catch your leg. This puts you on one leg and allows your opponent to do all sorts of nasty things, such as land strikes to your entire body or execute a takedown. The kick also makes you vulnerable to your opponent's right cross. If he throws a cross the instant you launch your round kick, his strike will land first because it's linear, which means it has less distance to travel to reach its target. However, round kicks to the midsection can be extremely effective in MMA when utilized properly. To prevent your opponent from catching your kick, it's best to set it up with punches. Personally, I like the lead hook or lead uppercut because both punches cause your opponent to lean backward, which disrupts his balance. Before he can reacquire his base and balance, you drive the kick into his midsection. The more punches you throw before launching the kick, the more success you will have. A great combination is the jab/cross/hook. The first two strikes elevate your opponent's guard in front of his face, and the hook sneaks around the side of his arms, strikes the side of his head, and moves his body directly into the kick. To avoid the infamous cross counter, it is important to step your lead foot toward the outside of your opponent's body. Deciding the angle of that step should be based upon your opponent's stance. Draw an imaginary line between the toes of his lead foot and the toes of his back foot, and then step your foot parallel to that angle. When you accomplish this, you not only remove your head from your centerline, but you also open your hips to throw a more powerful kick. To deliver that kick, bring your knee up and then quickly rotate your hips. The goal is not to snap your leg into your target, but rather use the rotation of your hips to turn your leg into a baseball bat that strikes through your target. It's not necessary to elevate your leg above your target and then chop down into it, as you would when throwing a leg kick. With mid kicks, you want to maintain a slight upward angle. This allows you to strike your shin into his last two ribs, both of which break easy, as well as catch your opponent's kidney with your foot. Just as with the shovel hook, you want to hit your target so that the energy travels diagonally through your opponent's body and exits his far shoulder. It is also extremely important to kick with your shin rather than your foot. If you throw a lot of kicks in a fight, chances are high that you'll strike your opponent's elbow at least once. If you kick with your foot, you can shatter a number of small bones, which will dramatically limit your mobility. The shin is a much stronger weapon, and it also inflicts more damage. While striking with the foot was effective back in the old kickboxing days due to the rules, it won't produce positive results in MMA competition.

1) Junie and I are in orthodox stances, searching for an opening to attack. 2) To set up a rear round kick to his midsection, I take a small outward step with my left foot. Notice how I point my left toes away from my opponent at a forty-five-degree angle. 3) Pivoting on the ball of my left foot, I rotate my hips and shoulders in a counterclockwise direction. Using my circular momentum, I whip my right leg off the mat toward Junie's midsection. 4) Continuing with my rotation, I whip the shin of my right leg into Junie's ribs. From here, I will allow the force of the impact to rebound my leg back into my fighting stance.

Low Round Kick (rear leg)

Directing the rear round kick to the outside of your opponent's lead leg is a lot safer than targeting his midsection or head because it's a much harder kick for him to catch. It's not as damaging of a strike, but if you land five or ten leg kicks during the course of a fight, you can severely restrict his movement. To prevent his abused lead leg from collapsing, he will often straighten it, which limits his ability to throw strikes, shoot in for takedowns, or defend against your attacks. It also pulls his focus down to the lower half of his body. Not wanting to take further abuse, the next time you throw a rear round kick, your opponent will often assume it is directed at his legs and drop his hands to defend against it. To make the most of his reaction, instead of directing the kick low, you throw it high to his unprotected midsection or face. The one thing you have to worry about when throwing low kicks is the cross. Instead of trying to check your kick, a lot of opponents will lean forward the instant your foot leaves the canvas and throw a powerful right straight down the middle. With a straight punch having to travel less distance than a circular kick, your opponent will often hit his target before you hit yours. To avoid such an outcome, it is very important to set your low kicks up with punches. Personally, I like to throw a jab to force my opponent to lean back, and then immediately follow up with a low round kick to the outside of his lead leg. Another option is to step to the outside of your opponent's rear leg prior to throwing the kick. This moves your head away from your opponent's line of fire, making it much harder for him to counter your kick. Whichever option you chose, it can be beneficial to reach your rear hand across your opponent's body as you kick. Although this doesn't allow you to generate as much power as when you throw your arm down to your side, it will help stifle your opponent's cross should he throw one.

Erich and I are in orthodox stances, searching for an opening to attack.

Keeping my right arm outstretched to prevent Erich from countering my kick with a right cross, I whip my hips in a counterclockwise direction and strike the outside of his lead leg using my right shin.

Seeing an opening to throw a rear round kick to the outside of Erich's lead leg, I step my right foot forward and then outside of his lead leg, shift my head toward my right side to remove it from his line of fire, reach my right arm forward to stifle his right cross, rotate my hips in a counterclockwise direction, and come up onto the ball of my right foot. It is important to notice how the toes of my lead foot are now pointing toward my left.

Anuwat Kaewsamrit

High Round Kick (rear leg)

Throwing a rear round kick to your opponent's head is exactly the same as throwing a rear round kick to his midsection—the only difference is the height of your target. For the best results, you want to pivot on the ball of your lead foot, rotate your hips and shoulder, and let your rear leg whip off the mat and into your target. The goal is to bring your leg above your opponent's lead shoulder, and then angle your shin downward so that it collides with the side of his neck and jaw. It can be a devastating kick when you land clean, but it is also a very risky kick to throw. Having to elevate your leg above your opponent's chest, your balance will be very weak, making it very easy for you to be toppled. Just as with the mid and low round kicks, you also have to watch out for your opponent's cross. Personally, I like to throw high round kicks when my opponent is backing up or immediately after breaking from the clinch.

1) My opponent and I are in orthodox fighting stances, searching for an opening to attack.

2) Seeing an opening to throw a round kick to my opponent's head, I pivot on my left foot, rotate my body in a counterclockwise direction, and let my right leg whip circularly off the mat. Instead of targeting my opponent's lead leg or ribs, I whip my leg up over his lead shoulder. To generate power for the kick, I throw my right arm behind me, and to protect myself from counterstrikes, I keep my left arm elevated.

Round Kick Sweep (rear leg)

It doesn't matter how long you have been training Muay Thai or if you've spent years kicking banana trees to harden your shins. When your opponent checks your kicks and your shin collides with his, it still hurts. If I'm up against an opponent who is a master at checking my low kicks, I'll employ this technique. It begins just as a regular low kick—by rotating your hips and pulling your rear foot off the mat. However, as your opponent lifts his lead leg to check your kick, you redirect your leg underneath his elevated foot and strike the calf muscle of his grounded leg. In addition to sweeping your opponent off his feet and causing his leg a fair amount of damage, it also messes with his mind. The next time you throw a low kick, he will think twice about checking, which allows you to once again direct your kick at the outside of his lead leg.

1) My opponent and I are in orthodox fighting stances, searching for an opening to attack. 2) Just as I would when throwing a regular round kick to the outside of my opponent's lead leg, I pivot on the ball of my left foot, rotate my hips and shoulders in a counterclockwise direction, and whip my right leg circularly off the mat. However, as my opponent lifts his left leg to check my kick, I redirect my kick underneath his elevated foot. 3) I crash my right shin into the calf of my opponent's grounded leg. The majority of the time landing the kick will not only cause damage to your opponent's grounded leg, but also sweep him off his feet.

Shawn Tompkins

Mid Round Kick (lead leg)

In this sequence I demonstrate how to throw a mid-level round kick with your lead leg. There are a couple of ways to accomplish this. The first method is to throw the kick directly from your stance, which I cover in the next sequence. The second method is to switch your stance prior to throwing the kick. This puts your lead foot behind you, allowing you to throw a more powerful kick. When employing this method, a lot of fighters like to throw the cross and then step their rear leg forward to switch their stance. Although some fighters use this effectively, it can be dangerous. As you now know, a lot of opponents will counter your kicks with a straight cross. When you step forward for the lead kick, you move directly into your opponent's power. If the forward momentum of his punch meets the forward momentum of your face, the results can be devastating. Personally, I teach my guys to switch their stance while standing in place. This is accomplished by taking a small upward hop, sliding the lead foot back, and the rear foot forward. The hop isn't dramatic. If your feet come more than an inch off the canvas, your transition will be slow and telegraphic. What are the benefits of the switch step? First, it will often make your opponent think you're retreating, causing him to move forward directly into your liver kick. Second, it allows you to acquire the proper distance between you and your opponent. If he is outside of range, you can move slightly forward with the switch step. If he is too close, you can also move slightly backward. It's still not a completely safe maneuver due to your opponent's right cross counter, so unless you're trying to bait your opponent into the kick, I recommend setting it up with punches. The jab is an excellent option because it forces your opponent to lean back, which in turn elevates his elbow away from his hip and exposes his ribs and liver.

My opponent and I are in orthodox fighting stances, searching for an opening to attack.

Although it is possible to throw a lead round kick directly from my stance, I reverse my stance to generate more power in the kick. To accomplish this, I hop upward, and while in midair, I bring my rear foot forward and my lead foot back.

Having reversed my stance, I pivot on the ball of my right foot, rotate my hips and shoulders in a clockwise direction, and whip my left shin circularly toward Junie's liver.

Continuing with my rotation, I crash my left shin into Junie's liver. Notice how I have kept my hands up to protect myself from counterstrikes.

Shawn Tompkins

Mid Round Kick (lead leg) (no switch step)

The second option for throwing the lead leg round kick to your opponent's midsection is to do so directly from your stance. You don't see this kick utilized very much in MMA because it makes it easy for a fighter to get knocked off balance, but it can be a devastating strike when in the hands of an experienced kickboxer who is precise with his movements. Where a lot of fighters go wrong is they throw this kick with the foot of their posted leg planted flat on the mat. In order for the kick to be effective, you must come up onto the ball of your planted foot. This allows you to rotate your hips. Without hip rotation, your kick not only lacks power, but it is also very difficult to quickly pull your leg back into your stance, which is mandatory to avoid your opponent's counterattacks. It is important to remember that every time you kick, all your balance is on one leg. The longer that leg remains off the ground, the more susceptible you will be to your opponent's strikes and takedowns. To be effective with this kick, you must master the hip rotation. To goal is to quickly snap your leg upward, deliver a hard blow, and then let your leg rebound off his body and whip back into your stance. However, even when executed flawlessly, this kick will make you vulnerable. To limit your chances of getting hit with a counterpunch or taken down, it's best to employ it in later rounds when your opponent's ability to react to your strikes has slowed considerably due to fatigue.

Junie and I are in orthodox fighting stances, searching for an opening to attack.

I slide my right foot up to my left foot. It is important to notice that I position my right foot so that my toes are pointing toward my right side. This primes my hips for a clockwise rotation and will allow me to throw a more powerful kick.

I rotate my hips in a clockwise direction and allow my left foot to be pulled off the mat.

Pivoting on the ball of my right foot, I continue my clockwise rotation and whip my left shin circularly into Junie's midsection. Notice how I have kept my arms up to protect myself from counterstrikes.

Anuwat Kaewsamrit

Inside Lead-Leg Kick

The inside lead leg kick is a very versatile strike. Offensively, it can be used to pull your opponent's focus low and disrupt his balance, which in turn sets you up to throw punches or elbows at his head. It's also an excellent strike to throw at the end of a combination to prevent your opponent from launching a counterattack. Defensively, it's a great way to hinder your opponent's ability to throw punches. As you learned in the punching section, a lot of weight is placed over the lead leg when punches are thrown. With this kick damaging the tendons on your opponent's lead leg, the more strikes you land, the harder it becomes for him to place weight on that leg to throw effective punches. The downside to utilizing this strike is that your opponent will often attempt to counter it with either a jab or cross. To prevent from getting hit, it is important to remove your head from his line of fire by stepping your rear foot to the outside of his lead leg prior to throwing the kick.

1) My opponent and I are in orthodox fighting stances, searching for an opening to attack. 2) To set up an inside lead leg kick, I step my right foot forward and to the outside of my opponent's lead leg. Notice how this primes my hips for a clockwise rotation and moves my head away from my opponent's line of fire. 3) Rotating my hips in a clockwise direction, I whip my left shin into the tendons running down the inside of my opponent's lead leg. Notice how I have thrown my left arm behind me to generate power in the kick. To protect myself from counterstrikes, I have kept my right arm elevated.

Uppercut Elbow (rear arm) *Shawn Tompkins*

The uppercut elbow is a great tool to have when in close range. A lot of times when you have your opponent pinned up against the cage and are attacking his legs or hips for a takedown, he will defend by spreading his legs and leaning his upper body over your back. If you realize that his defenses are too strong and you're not going to get the takedown, a good option is to nudge his body away from you using your lead forearm, quickly increase your elevation, and land an uppercut elbow to his chin using your rear arm. When you initiate this break from the clinch, you're usually one step ahead of your opponent, and with his body already leaning forward, there is a good chance that you will land clean to his jaw with the strike. It's important to quickly reestablish your guard after landing the strike, but usually when you land the uppercut elbow, your opponent will have to gather his senses and reestablish his base before retaliating with strikes of his own.

1) Junie and I are in orthodox fighting stances, searching for an opening to attack. 2) To set up the rear uppercut elbow, I take a small outward step with my left foot, come up onto the ball of my right foot, rotate my hips in a counterclockwise direction, and open my right hand. 3) Continuing with my counterclockwise rotation, I reach my right hand behind my right ear and drive my right elbow upward into Junie's chin, lifting his head.

Anuwat Kaewsamrit

Uppercut Elbow (lead arm)

The lead uppercut elbow is not as powerful as the rear uppercut elbow, but it's a very quick strike that allows you to close the distance, lift your opponent's chin, and often secure the Muay Thai clinch. The key to success is not telegraphing your strike. From your fighting stance, step your lead foot forward and bring your lead elbow directly up into your opponent's chin. If you drop your elbow to generate more power in your strike, your opponent will most likely bring his arms together to protect his centerline.

| My opponent and I are in orthodox fighting stances, searching for an opening to attack. | I step my left foot forward so that it is positioned between my opponent's legs. | Rotating my hips in a clockwise direction, I come up onto the ball of my right foot and drive my left elbow upward into my opponent's chin. |

Over-the-Top Elbow   *Shawn Tompkins*

Just like the uppercut elbow, the over-the-top elbow is best utilized when you have your opponent pressed up against the cage. When in this position, your opponent will often be concerned about the takedown. Unable to defend your shots by sprawling due to the fence, he will lower his hands to catch your body. The instant you see this, throw the over-the-top elbow so that it slides down his forehead and face. When executed properly, chances are you will catch his eyebrow or nose as your elbow travels downward. This will usually open a diagonal cut, which is a kind that tends to bleed profusely and is difficult to close.

1) Junie and I are fighting in close range. Both of us are in orthodox stances. 2) Rotating my hips in a counterclockwise direction, I elevate my right elbow and separate Junie's guard using my left hand. 3) Continuing with my counterclockwise rotation, I come up onto the ball of my right foot and drive my right elbow downward. The goal is to slide the tip of your elbow down your opponent's forehead and face to open a cut.

Shawn Tompkins

Side Elbow (rear arm)

Landing a powerful elbow strike is an excellent way to open a cut on your opponent's face or head, and there is no elbow strike more powerful than the rear side elbow. A lot of people feel that opening a cut is a cheap route to victory, but I disagree. It's simply another way to win a fight. There are a couple of ways to set up the side elbow. You can box your way into close range and then throw the elbow, or you can throw the elbow while tied up with your opponent in the clinch. Both are somewhat risky when up against a good Greco-Roman wrestler. Boxing your way into the side elbow puts you in very close range, which can potentially allow your opponent to tie you up, and in order to throw the side elbow from the clinch, you must create space between you and your opponent, which can potentially allow him to establish a dominant hold. Personally, I teach my fighters to primarily use the rear side elbow when they have their opponent pressed up against the cage because their mobility is limited. When in this position, there are a couple of ways to set it up. You can establish the dirty boxing clinch by wrapping one hand around the back of your opponent's head, and then use that control to pull his head toward the ground. As he resists this pressure and pulls his head upward, you throw the rear side elbow with your opposite arm. Another way is to deliver several hard knee strikes to your opponent's body. After the first shot, there is a good chance your opponent will drop his arms to block your strikes, creating a clear path to land the rear side elbow to his face. If your opponent has his arms glued to the sides of his head, which can prevent the rear side elbow from landing clean, a good tactic is to force his arms downward. A lot of fighters will accomplish this by grabbing their opponent's lead arm with their lead hand, pull it downward, and then throw the rear side elbow. However, I recommend grabbing your opponent's lead arm with your rear hand. As you force his hand downward, you step forward, rotate your hips, and slide your rear elbow over his arm and into his face. Executing the trap with the same arm you throw your elbow with can be very elusive. If you've watched a lot of MMA fights, you'll see fighters use this technique all the time while in their opponent's guard. It works just as effectively when on your feet. Deciding where to target your rear side elbow depends upon your goals in the fight. If you want to open a cut, you want to graze the tip of your elbow across your opponent eyebrow or the side of his cheek. If your goal is to score a knockout, crash the tip of your elbow into his temple or jaw.

Junie and I are in orthodox fighting stances, searching for an opening to attack.

With Junie's guard slightly dropped, I set up a rear side elbow by stepping my left foot forward and to the outside of his lead leg, rotate my hips in a counterclockwise direction, come up onto the ball of my right foot, and elevate my right elbow

Continuing to rotate my hips in a counterclockwise direction, I whip my right elbow circularly into the left side of Junie's jaw. It is important to notice that both of my hands are open. My left hand is protecting my face from counterstrikes, and my right hand is angled in toward my body.

Shawn Tompkins

Side Elbow (lead arm)

The lead side elbow is an excellent strike to utilize when up against an opponent who applies constant forward pressure. To execute it in such a situation, move your lower body toward him while at the same time rotating your hips and shoulders circularly. The forward movement is important because it allows you to increase the force behind your strike, and the circular movement of your hips and shoulders is important because it allows you to whip your elbow horizontally into your target. The strike doesn't pack as much power as a rear elbow, making it difficult to knock your opponent out with it. For this reason, it is important to focus on opening a cut by slicing the tip of your elbow across your opponent's eyebrow or cheek.

1) Junie and I are in orthodox fighting stances, searching for an opening to attack. 2) With Junie's guard slightly dropped, I see an opening to throw a lead side elbow. To set up the strike, I take a small outward step with my lead foot and rotate my body in a counterclockwise direction, just as I would when evading my opponent's jab or setting up a lead hook. 3) Elevating my left elbow, I unleash my spring-loaded hips by rotating them in a clockwise direction. As I pivot on the ball of my left foot, I whip my left elbow circularly into the right side of Junie's jaw. It is important to notice that both of my hands are open. My right hand is protecting my face, and my left hand is angled in toward my body.

Anuwat Kaewsamrit

Spinning Back Elbow

Although the spinning back elbow is a very flashy move, it is responsible for countless knockouts in Muay Thai competition. To execute it, step your lead foot across your body and to the outside of your opponent's lead leg. This momentarily turns your back to your opponent, which gives him an opportunity to launch an attack, so it is important to be quick with your movements. The instant your foot touches down, rotate your body circularly and whip your rear elbow around and into the side of your opponent's face. The downside to this technique is that if your opponent's guard is up, your elbow will often crash into his forearms. For the best results, you want to utilize it when your opponent's arms are down, which usually occurs when he is dazed or tired or when he steps into close range in an attempt to tie you up in the clinch.

My opponent and I are standing in orthodox stances, searching for an opening to attack.

I step my left foot forward and to the outside of my opponent's lead leg.

Distributing my weight onto my left leg, I rotate in a clockwise direction and whip my right elbow circularly toward my opponent's face.

Continuing with my clockwise rotation, I thrust my right elbow into the right side of my opponent's face.

Straight Knee (lead leg)

The lead knee is a lot like the lead round kick in that it can be thrown after stepping your rear foot forward, immediately after executing a switch step, or directly from your stance. In the sequence below, I demonstrate how to throw it directly from your stance. The mechanics of the strike require you to shift your weight onto your back leg, which makes it easy for your opponent to push you off balance, so it's best utilized when tied up in the clinch. Personally, I like to set it up by establishing double collar ties, which is often called the Muay Thai clinch. When you establish this hold on a wrestler, a lot of the time he will drop his elevation to attack your legs. As he lowers his level, bring your lead knee straight up into his solar plexus. The lead knee is not as powerful as the rear knee, so it is important that you throw it with 100 percent power. Your recovery is also extremely important. If your knee doesn't knock your opponent out, there is a good chance that he will continue to drive forward for your legs. To avoid the takedown, pivot to the outside of your opponent's body and pull his head in the same direction. This will shatter his balance, not only making it difficult for him to complete the takedown, but also creating an opportunity for you to follow up with more knee strikes. When throwing the lead knee from the outside, it is very important to set it up with punches. Just as with the lead round kick, a lot of fighters like to throw the cross, step their lead foot forward to switch their stance, and then throw the lead knee. However, this poses the same problems as when stepping forward to throw the lead round kick. Your opponent's most common reaction will be to throw a punch, and with you moving directly into his power, there is a good chance he will knock you out if he lands. A much better approach is to employ several punches to stretch out your opponent's ribs and get him to lean back, execute a switch step, and then deliver the knee. As I already mentioned, you don't have to execute a switch step in your exact location. You can use it to either move forward or backward, depending upon your opponent's range. As far as a target, you can go to your opponent's head, mid-section, or thigh. Personally, I like to drive the tip of my lead knee into my opponent's liver and his bottom two ribs.

Junie and I are standing in orthodox stances, searching for an opening to attack.

To set up a straight lead knee, I shoot my right arm forward just as if I were throwing a cross, but instead of striking Junie's face, I reach behind his head and cup my hand around the back of his neck.

I pull Junie's head down using my right hand, and then place my left hand on the top of his head to acquire more leverage.

Keeping Junie's head down using my hands, I elevate my left knee.

Still pulling down on Junie's head, I lean back and drive my knee horizontally into his solar plexus.

Straight Knee (rear leg)

KNEES

Anytime you lift a leg off the mat your balance is jeopardized. This is especially true with knee strikes because they are thrown from such close proximity to your opponent. To evade your knee strike and knock you to the mat, your opponent simply has to reach his arms forward and give you a little shove. To prevent such an outcome, I will usually latch on to my opponent's head prior to throwing a knee strike. In the sequence below, I accomplish this by shooting my rear arm forward, just as I would when throwing a cross. However, instead of punching my opponent in the face, I reach my hand past the far side of his head and hook my hand around the back of his neck. In addition to stabilizing my body, assuming a cross grip on my opponent's head also makes it difficult for him to launch a counterstrike. Once I have the control established, I pull his head down and drive my rear knee upward into his midsection.

My opponent and I are in orthodox stances, searching for an opening to attack.

To set up a straight rear knee, I step my left foot forward.

I shoot my right arm forward just as I would when throwing a cross, but instead of striking my opponent's face, I reach my hand past the right side of his head and wrap my fingers around the back of his neck.

Pulling my opponent's head downward using my right hand, I elevate my right knee and then drive it horizontally into his midsection.

I pull my leg back into my fighting stance and then release control of his head.

Shawn Tompkins

Slipping the Jab

In this sequence I demonstrate how to slip a jab when you and your opponent are in the same fighting stance. The movement is quite simple—as your opponent's fist comes at you, slightly rotate your shoulders and move your head to the outside of his striking arm. When done correctly, you completely avoid contact with your opponent's strike. Although it's certainly possible to block the jab, which is done frequently in boxing, it is a lot more risky in MMA due to the small gloves. It is impossible to protect your entire face when you cover up, so your opponent's fist is able to slip through one of the gaps. Even when you do manage to block the jab with your arms, you take damage. Over the course of a fight, blocking fifty jabs with your forearms can add up and slow your punches. Slipping is vastly superior for several reasons. First, you make your opponent miss. When you expect to make contact with something and then don't, it disrupts your balance. Second, a proper slip gives you a dominant angle of attack. With your ear positioned to the outside of your opponent's lead arm, it becomes very easy to attack with a take-down by either shooting for his legs or wrapping your arms around his body. However, there are some very crucial elements that go along with executing a proper slip. The most important one is not to exaggerate your movement. Bruce Lee was a big believer in this, and so I am. If you can slip your opponent's jab by moving your head slightly to the outside, why dip your head dramatically downward. It accomplishes the same goal of allowing you to evade the punch, but it takes you longer to counter with an attack of your own and makes you vulnerable to knees and kicks. Another key element is protecting the side of your face closest to your opponent. The majority of the time your opponent will follow the jab with a cross, and if you weren't able to close the distance for whatever reason, you will need that inside arm elevated to protect your face. To help you ingrain this movement into your subconscious, I recommend drilling in three stages as often as possible. The first stage is to practice the movement solo. If your gym has pads on the wall, position your centerline along the crease that separates them. For several minutes warm up by repeatedly slipping your head to the outside of that crease. Next, grab a partner and practice the exact same movement, but this time have him throw slow jabs at your face. Finally, take things up a notch by slipping his jabs and then quickly closing the distance to tie him up in the clinch.

Junie and I are in orthodox stances, searching for an opening to attack.

Junie throws a jab toward my face.

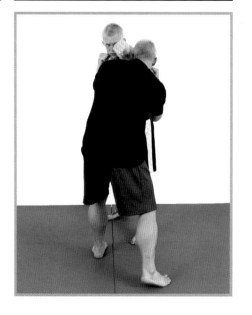

To evade Junie's jab, I rotate my shoulders slightly in a clockwise direction and move my head toward my right side. Having moved my head away from my centerline, Junie's jab passes by the left side of my head.

Shawn Tompkins

Slipping the Cross

Slipping the cross has all the benefits of slipping the jab, but it can be a difficult movement for new students. Everyone knows the cross is a very powerful punch, and when it comes at you, your natural instinct is to turn away from it. Although this might feel right, it is the completely wrong reaction. Instead, you want to rotate your body toward the punch and the outside of your opponent's outstretched arm. Just as with the jab, this allows you to evade the punch completely. It also creates the opportunity to launch a number of attacks. The movement involved with your outward rotation is similar to the movement you make when throwing the overhand right, making it easy to combine the two into one fluid motion. With one of your opponent's arms away from his face, there is a good chance that your overhand will land right on his chin. If you chose not to strike as you make your rotation, you still have a chance to strike immediately after. With your hips already spring-loaded with your defensive movement, you can throw a lead hook directly over your opponent's outstretched arm and to the side of his jaw or you can throw the hook underneath his arm and to his liver. If grappling is more your thing, slipping the cross also positions you perfectly to slide your body forward underneath your opponent's cross and attack either his legs or hips with a takedown.

Junie and I are standing in an orthodox stance, searching for an opening to attack.

Junie throws a right cross. To evade his strike, I shift my weight onto my left leg, rotate my hips and shoulders in a counterclockwise direction, come up onto the ball of my right foot, and shift my head toward my left side.

As I continue with my counterclockwise rotation, Junie's cross slips past the right side of my head.

Parrying the Jab

When parrying a punch, instead of moving your body to avoid all contact with your opponent's strike, as you do when executing a slip, you place a hand on his arm and redirect it away from your body. Deciding whether to use a slip or a jab should be based upon your goal in the fight. Slipping the jab does not tie up either arm, which allows you to immediately launch a counterstrike. As a result, it's best employed when you want to keep the fight more of a boxing or kickboxing match. When you put your hands on your opponent's arm to redirect it, you momentarily lose your ability to strike with that hand. However, by latching on to his wrist you gain control of a part of his body, which in turn allows you to shift the fight into more of a grappling match. So as a rule of thumb, use the slip when you want to keep the fight in the striking arena, and use the parry when you want to transition into the grappling arena.

Junie and I are in orthodox stances, searching for an opening to attack.

As Junie throws a jab, I rotate my hips and shoulders in a counterclockwise direction, come up onto the ball of my right foot, and place my right hand on the left side of his arm to redirect it to the left of my head.

As I redirect Junie's jab to my left, his arm sails past the left side of my head. Notice how I have kept my left arm elevated.

Parrying the Cross
Shawn Tompkins

In this sequence I demonstrate how to parry a cross when you and your opponent are in the same fighting stance. Just as with parrying the jab, it requires you to put a hand on your opponent's arm. Although this sometimes hinders your ability to counter with strikes, it makes it easier to obtain wrist control and transition into the clinch or a takedown. However, it is important to remember that your opponent will not keep his arm outstretched for long. If your goal is to score a takedown or establish a clinch when executing the parry, immediately grab your opponent's arm and then close the distance between your bodies.

Junie and I are in orthodox stances, searching for an opening to attack.

As Junie throws a right cross, I rotate my hips and shoulders in a clockwise direction and redirect his arm toward the right of my head using my left hand.

As I redirect Junie's cross, his arm sails past the right side of my head. Notice how I have kept my right arm elevated.

Shawn Tompkins

Evade Cross with the Drift

In this sequence I demonstrate how to utilize "the drift" to evade your opponent's cross. It's a very deceptive technique because instead of raising your arms to block the punch or slipping to the outside of his striking arm, you simply lean back. It is important not to dramatically jerk your head backward the instant you spot the cross because it will alert your opponent to your intentions. Instead of continuing forward with the cross, he may retract his punch, wait until you off-balance yourself with your backward motion, and then capitalize on your awkward positioning with an alternate strike. For the best results, you want to keep your face as close to your opponent's advancing fist as possible to instill confidence in him and cause him to overextend his arm. The instant his arm reaches its full extension, you want to follow his fist as he pulls it back into his stance and counter with a punch of your own. If you wait until your opponent retracts his fist before you move your body toward him, there is a very good chance that you will run into a secondary punch. For this reason, the drift is a very advanced technique, but it is definitely worth taking some time to master. Muay Thai kickboxers use the drift all the time, especially with high kicks. Instead of trying to catch their opponent's leg with their arm, they simply lean back and let the kick sail by their head. Before their opponent can reestablish his base and balance, they come flying forward and attack his exposed back with a kick of their own. The best piece of advice I have on the drift is to get a feeling for your opponent's range before using it. Some fighters have a longer reach than others, and with the technique requiring you to be extremely close to your opponent's advancing fist, you must know the exact extension of his arm. The majority of the time, I advise my fighters to save the drift until the later rounds of a fight.

Junie and I are in orthodox stances, searching for an opening to attack.

Junie throws a right cross at my face. To evade his strike, I distribute a larger portion of my weight onto my rear leg and lean my upper body backward. Notice how I keep both arms up to protect my face.

As Junie pulls his arm back into his stance, I lean forward and follow his fist with my upper body. The goal is to launch a counterstrike before your opponent can follow up his cross with another strike.

While Junie is still pulling his cross arm back into his stance, I rotate my hips in a counterclockwise direction, come up onto the ball of my right foot, and throw a cross at his chin.

Bob and Weave

Utilizing the bob and weave to evade your opponent's hooks is very effective in boxing, but when you employ this evasive technique in MMA, there is a good chance that you will bob and weave directly into a kick or knee. The majority of the time it's better to utilize the drift to evade the hook, but I still drill the bob and weave with my fighters because it can come in very handy in a couple of situations. The first situation is when you're up against a fighter who throws a lot of hooks but very rarely throws kicks or knees. Instead of constantly using the drift to evade his strikes, you drop your elevation, weave underneath his punch, and then use the rotation of your body to deliver a hard hook to his face. I wouldn't recommend using this technique several times in a row because your opponent might switch up his attacks and deliver a kick or knee, but pulling it out a couple of times in a round is a great way to throw off your opponent. The other time the bob and weave comes in handy is when you're pressed up against the fence and your opponent is attacking with a multipunch combination. Unable to retreat backward due to the fence, employing the bob and weave can save you from taking a lot of punishment. However, when in this scenario it is absolutely mandatory to use the bob and weave to improve your positioning. If you attempt to bob and weave all day long, eventually your opponent will figure out where you are weaving and alter the course of his strikes. To prevent this from happening, pay close attention to your opponent's body positioning. If he's throwing a multipunch combination, chances are there will be moments where his balance is compromised. The instant you see a weakness in his base, drop your level, obtain control of his legs, and either execute a takedown or circle off the cage.

Junie and I are standing in close range. Both of us are in orthodox fighting stances.

Junie rotates his body in a clockwise direction to set up a rear hook.

As Junie throws a rear hook, I begin dropping my elevation by bending my knees and sinking my hips. Notice how I have not leaned forward and I've kept both of my hands up to protect my face.

4

I continue to drop my elevation so that my thighs are almost parallel with the ground. At the same time, I shift a larger percentage of my weight onto my left leg, come up onto the ball of my right foot, and weave my body toward my left side.

5

As Junie's hook sails over the top of my head, I rotate my body in a counterclockwise direction and rise back up into my fighting stance. Notice how my actions have spring-loaded my hips.

6

While Junie is trying to reestablish his fighting stance after missing his strike, I rotate my hips and shoulders in a clockwise direction, shift a larger percentage of my weight onto my rear leg, pivot on the ball of my left foot, and throw a lead hook toward the side of his jaw.

7

Keeping my right foot planted on the mat, I continue to rotate in a clockwise direction and pivot on my left foot. As my fist nears its target, I rotate my fist so my palm is facing the ground and then strike the side of Junie's jaw with the knuckles of my index and middle fingers. As I mentioned in the introduction to the hook, you have two options for landing the punch. You can keep your palm facing toward you, which produces more push, or you can rotate your fist so your palm faces the mat, which produces more snap.

Shawn Tompkins

Deflecting the Front Kick

Although there aren't a lot of MMA fighters who utilize the front kick, the few fighters who have taken the time to master this strike utilize it all of the time. A perfect example is Gina Carano. As I mentioned earlier, she concludes almost every combination with a push kick to off-balance her opponent. Absorbing one of these shots is a nuisance—absorbing half a dozen of them in a single round can cause you serious damage. To avoid taking unnecessary abuse, I demonstrate how to evade the push kick in the sequence below. When you spot the kick coming, the first step is to rotate your body so that your lead shoulder is pointing toward your opponent. This makes your body as narrow as possible, increasing the chance that the kick misses entirely or slides off your side. The next step is to gain control of your opponent's leg by grabbing his ankle. If you and your opponent are in the same fighting stance and he throws the kick with his lead leg, you grab his ankle with your lead hand. If you are in the same fighting stance and he throws the kick with his rear leg, grab his ankle with your rear hand. Obtaining the proper grip is extremely important because it allows you to move to the outside of your opponent's kick. Just as with the jab and cross, you never want to move to the inside of your opponent's strike because you will move directly into his power. As you will see in the sequence below, moving to the outside of your opponent's leg exposes his back, allowing you to strike or execute a takedown with very little risk.

Junie and I are in orthodox stances, searching for an opening to attack.

Junie elevates his lead knee toward his chest, alerting me to the fact that he is about to throw a lead leg push kick.

As Junie rockets the ball of his lead foot toward my midsection, I shift my weight onto my rear leg, rotate my body in a clockwise direction to make my body as narrow as possible, and then drop my left arm and cup the outside of his leg with my left hand. It is important to notice that I have kept my right hand up to protect my face.

Once I have made contact with Junie's leg, I shift my weight onto my lead leg, rotate my body in a counterclockwise direction, and redirect his leg to the outside of my body. Notice how this disrupts his base and balance.

I release Junie's left leg and elevate my left arm to protect my face. At the same time, I continue with my counterclockwise rotation and throw a right cross toward the left side of his jaw.

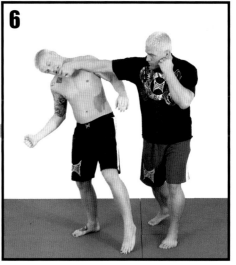

Continuing with my rotation, I land a cross to the left side of Junie's jaw.

Shawn Tompkins

Low Check

Low kicks are very popular in MMA, and you need to learn how to deal with them. If you don't have the time needed to evade the strike by moving out of the way, there are two primary methods of defense. The first is to step into the kick and cut it off. For example, if your opponent throws a rear round kick at your lead leg, you step your lead foot toward your opponent's kick. Although this requires you to absorb the strike on your leg, the goal is to make contact and stuff the kick before it can generate a lot of power. To make your opponent pay, you throw a right cross to your opponent's face as you step forward. While the low kick takes many shots to inflict fight-ending damage, the cross can end a fight in a single blow. It's a trade-off, but usually a worthwhile one. In the sequence below I demonstrate the second method, which is to check the kick. In order to utilize a proper check, you want to elevate your leg so that your opponent's advancing shin collides with your shin. To achieve this, point the toes of your checking leg toward your opponent's kick. If you point your toes forward instead, there is a good chance the kick will blast right through your checking leg and sweep your opposite leg off the mat, causing you to fall to the floor. While checking certainly has its place, it is important to realize that it too is a trade-off due to the bone-on-bone contact. As a result, I will usually instruct my fighters to utilize the first method whenever possible. The only time I instruct them to check low kicks is when they are off balance or up against a fighter who has excellent timing with their kicks, making it difficult to counter with a cross. To be a well-rounded fighter, I recommend practicing them both. I also recommend conditioning your shins to take the abuse. I hear a lot of new fighters talking about rolling coke bottles up and down their shins to toughen them, but this will only damage your legs. The single best way to deaden the nerves in your shins is to kick a leather heavy bag as often as possible.

1) Junie and I are in orthodox stances, searching for an opening to attack. 2) Junie takes an outward step with his lead leg, alerting me to the fact that he is most likely gearing up to throw a rear round kick. Immediately I shift my weight onto my right leg and come up onto the ball of my left foot. 3) As Junie follows through with a rear round kick, I elevate my left knee so that my shin is angled toward the outside of my body at a forty-five-degree angle. This allows me to catch his shin with my shin and block his kick. It is important to mention that you do not want to lift your knee so that it is pointing straight at your opponent because his kick will strike the side of your calf, causing damage to the muscles and tendons. You always want to angle your knee toward the outside of your body at a forty-five-degree angle to ensure that you properly block the kick and cause your opponent damage.

Mid Check (option 1) *Shawn Yarborough*

In this sequence I demonstrate how to check a round kick aimed at your midsection. Just as with the low kick, you want to elevate your leg off the mat and angle your knee outward so that your opponent's shin collides with your shin. The only difference with the mid kick is that you elevate your leg slightly higher, as well as position your elbow to the outside of your checking leg. This last nuance creates a barrier on one whole side of your body, which can prevent you from taking a hard blow should your opponent redirect his kick to your head at the last moment.

Erich pivots on his left foot and throws a rear round kick at my ribs. To check his kick, I elevate my leg, point my knee toward the outside of my body at a forty-five-degree angle, and position my left elbow to the outside of my left leg. Having executed a perfect check, his shin collides into mine. Although the impact causes us both damage, he is worse for the wear.

Mid Check (option 2)

The majority of Muay Thai kickboxers check a round kick aimed at their midsection just as they do a round kick aimed at their leg—by lifting their leg and catching the kick on their shin. Although this is certainly an option in MMA, every time you lift a foot off the mat, you become susceptible to takedowns. For example, if every time your opponent kicks you lift your leg to check it, he might fake a kick to generate this reaction and then shoot in for a takedown instead. To avoid this possible outcome, I prefer to check mid-level round kicks using my arms. However, with the mid-level round kick being one of the strongest kicks in your opponent's arsenal, it is important that you move into the strike and catch his leg before he can generate maximum velocity with his kick. This also puts you in punching range, which allows you to immediately counter with a hook or overhand. As long as you launch your counterstrike while your opponent is still on one foot, there is a strong chance that you will catch him right on the button. As I mentioned before, each time your opponent throws a strike, you want to make him pay. This technique is an excellent way to accomplish this goal when dealing with mid-level round kicks. Once you've used it successfully several times in a fight, your opponent will grow fearful of throwing mid-level round kicks. It breaks him mentally. He might still throw one occasionally, but fearing the painful repercussions, it will not be with the same commitment.

1) Junie and I are in orthodox stances, and he steps his lead leg to the outside of his body, alerting me to the fact that he is about to throw a rear round kick. **2)** Junie throws his kick toward my midsection. Although I can check the mid round kick just as I did the low round kick, it would jeopardize my balance and make it difficult to immediately retaliate with a counterstrike. Instead, I take an outward step with my lead foot, rotate my body in a counterclockwise direction, and position the outside of my forearms in front of my body. The goal with moving into the kick is to make contact with your opponent's leg before he can generate maximum velocity with his kick. **3)** Having rotated my body in a counterclockwise direction, Junie's shin collides with the outside of my forearms. It is important to mention that if you do not rotate your body, your opponent's kick will be absorbed with just one of your arms, increasing the risk of injury.

High Block   *Shawn Tompkins*

In this sequence I demonstrate how to block a rear round kick aimed at your head. Although you don't rotate your body into the kick as you would when it is directed at your midsection, you still want to absorb the strike on both of your arms to reduce the risk of injury. To accomplish this, elevate your near arm to catch your opponent's shin. At the same time, cross your far arm behind your near arm and wrap the back of your hand over your ear. With your palm facing outward, it will catch your opponent's foot.

1) Junie and I are in orthodox stances, searching for an opening to attack. **2)** Junie throws a rear round kick at my head. To block the strike, I elevate my left arm so that my forearm is perpendicular with the mat and rotate my hand so that my palm is facing my opponent. At the same time, I move my right arm across my body and place the back of my hand over my left ear. Assuming this positioning will allow me to catch his shin on my left forearm and his foot with my right palm.

Shawn Yarborough

Checking Inside Lead-Leg Kick

Blocking a round kick aimed at the inside of your lead leg requires very little movement. All you do is pull your lead foot off the mat and move your leg into the kick, almost as if you too are throwing an inside leg kick. You don't want to blast your leg into your opponent's leg, but you want to meet his leg before he can generate full velocity with his kick. Just as when checking any kick, you want to make contact with the blade of your shin to minimize the damage you take. Once the kick is checked, it is important to immediately drop your foot back to the mat and launch a counter while your opponent is still balanced on one leg. If your opponent has a long reach, a cross is an excellent option, and if he is within close range or has a short reach, a rear side elbow is a great way to cause some damage.

Erich throws a round kick at the inside of my lead leg. Immediately I elevate my left foot off the mat, but instead of angling my knee toward the outside of my body, I angle it toward the inside of my body. This allows me to catch his leg with my shin.

Shawn Tompkins

Blocking a Knee Strike to the Body

There are a lot of fighters who have mastered knee strikes, especially those who are wary of the fight going to the ground. Every time you drop your level to shoot in, they throw a knee strike to prevent you from achieving your goal. To avoid taking abuse, a good tactic is to greet his elevating knee with an elbow strike using the technique below. In addition to blocking his strike, you also inflict a fair amount of pain. When you land clean, it damages the nerves on the inside of his leg, often causing his leg to freeze up. If your goal is to take the fight to the ground, this presents a perfect opportunity to shoot in for a takedown.

1) Junie and I are in orthodox stances, searching for an opening to attack. 2) Junie throws a rear knee at my midsection. To block the strike, I move into the strike by shifting my weight onto my lead leg and rotating my body in a counterclockwise direction. As his knee approaches, I use my rotation to drive my right elbow against the inside of his right thigh. Not only does this redirect his knee to the outside of my body, but it also damages the nerves of his leg. Before he can pull his leg back into his stance, I will follow up with either strikes or a takedown.

Redirecting a Knee Strike to Body

In this sequence I demonstrate how to deflect a straight knee aimed at your body, which not only allows you to avoid the strike, but also disrupts your opponent's balance. The key to success with this technique is stepping back and shifting your weight onto your rear leg the instant you see the knee coming toward you. This will often cause your opponent to overextend his strike, making it much easier to push his leg to the side using your hand. Once his back is turned, an excellent option is to throw a side elbow as demonstrated below. However, the one thing you must watch out for when utilizing this technique is the spinning back elbow. The instant you expose your opponent's back, he will realize his vulnerability. A lot of times, he will continue to rotate his body and throw a spinning elbow in the hopes of catching you as you come forward.

Erich and I are in orthodox stances, searching for an opening to attack.

Erich shifts his weight onto his lead leg and comes up onto the ball of his rear foot. This tells me he is either going to throw a rear round kick or a rear knee.

As Erich elevates his rear knee, I step my rear foot backward to create distance, shift my weight onto my rear leg, and come up onto the ball of my lead foot. If he were to throw a kick, I would be in the perfect position to execute a check. In this case, however, he throws a rear knee toward my midsection. Having shifted my weight backward, my body is out of range. This allows me to place my left hand on the outside of his right knee and force it toward my right side.

I push Erich's right knee toward my right side, causing his body to rotate in a counterclockwise direction.

I step my left foot forward, slide my right foot toward my left foot to maintain my fighting stance, and then rotate my body in a counterclockwise direction and throw a rear side elbow toward the right side of Erich's neck.

Continuing with my counterclockwise rotation, I deliver a rear side elbow to Erich's neck. It is important to notice that I have kept my left arm elevated to protect myself from a spinning back elbow.

Forrest Griffin

Jab - Cross to Body - Hook to Head

This is a very basic combination that follows the low/high principle, which is that you should alternate your strikes between your opponent's lower and upper body. From within striking range, I begin by throwing a jab at my opponent's face to get him to elevate his arms. Next, I throw a cross into his abdomen, causing him to drop his arms to protect his midsection. With his head once again exposed, I conclude the combination by throwing a lead hook to the side of his jaw. The nice thing about this combination is that each punch flows into the next. By throwing the jab, my hips get spring-loaded for the cross, and by throwing the cross, my hips get spring-loaded for the lead hook. Once you conclude the combination, your opponent will most likely fire back, so it is important to either back up or circle around his body.

1 Lance and I are in the same fighting stance, searching for an opening to attack.

2 I throw a jab to force Lance to elevate his arms and protect his head.

3 With Lance's arms elevated, I rotate my hips in a counterclockwise direction, come up onto the ball of my rear foot, and throw a cross to his body.

4 As Lance drops his arms to protect his body, I shift my weight onto my rear leg, pivot on the ball of my lead foot, rotate my hips in a clockwise direction, and throw a lead hook to the right side of his head.

5 Having concluded my combination, I immediately back away from Lance to avoid his counters.

Shawn Tompkins

Cross - Hook - Cross

This is an excellent combination to use to cover distance and get your opponent to back up. Personally, I like to employ it when my opponent is nearing the cage or ropes. By throwing the initial cross, I force him to lean back. Before he can recover his balance, I follow up with a lead hook. Unable to lean back further to avoid the hook, he will usually step back into the cage or ropes, making it very difficult for him to evade the second cross. I have my students who are primarily wrestlers train this combination all the time, but instead of having them conclude the combination with the second cross, I have them immediately drop their level and shoot in for a takedown. Being rattled from strikes and backed against the cage wall, it will be very difficult for their opponent to defend against it.

Junie and I are in the same fighting stance, searching for an opening to attack.

I take a small outward step with my lead foot, come up onto the ball of my rear foot, and begin rotating my hips in a counterclockwise direction.

Continuing to rotate my hips and shoulders in a counterclockwise direction, I throw a right cross at Junie's chin.

With Junie's balance disrupted from my cross, I sit my weight onto my rear leg, pivot on the ball of my lead foot, rotate my hips in a clockwise direction, and throw a lead hook toward the right side of his head.

Junie leans back further to evade my hook, disrupting his balance even more.

Before Junie can reestablish his base and balance, I plant my lead foot on the mat and rotate my hips and shoulders in a counter-clockwise direction.

Still rotating, I come up onto the ball of my rear foot and throw a right cross to Junie's chin. Unable to lean further back to evade my cross, he gets hit directly on the chin.

Forrest Griffin

Cross - Hook - Cross - Slip to Outside

This combination consists of a cross, a lead hook, and then another cross. When you throw two power punches in a single combination, your opponent will most likely have one of three reactions. He will drop because you just knocked him out (the best one, obviously), he will back up, or he will hold his ground and immediately counter. If he chooses the last of these options, it is important to get out of the way. Personally, I like to drop my elevation to avoid his strikes and then weave to the outside of his body to remove myself from the danger zone. It's possible to remain in the pocket and counter your opponent's counters, but that takes excellent timing. For mere mortals, I recommend getting the hell out of the way.

Lance and I are in the same fighting stance, searching for an opening to attack.

Rotating my hips in a counterclockwise direction, I come up onto the ball of my rear foot and throw a cross to Lance's face.

Shifting my weight onto my rear leg, I pivot on the ball of my lead foot, rotate my hips in a clockwise direction, and throw a lead hook to the right side of Lance's face.

Shifting my weight forward again, I rotate my hips in a counterclockwise direction, come up onto the ball of my rear foot, and throw another cross at Lance's face.

Having struck Lance with several punches, he will most likely retaliate with punches of his own. To avoid getting hit with his counters, I step my rear foot to the outside of his lead leg, drop my elevation by bending at the knees, and weave my body toward my right side. This is an excellent technique if you're like me and your timing is far from perfect. Knowing I most likely won't be able to react in time should my opponent counter, I utilize this technique to create separation.

Having shifted my body to the outside of Lance's body, I am relatively safe from his counters and increase my elevation.

Forrest Griffin

Lead Hook - Cross - Outside Pivot - Hook

This combination begins with a lead hook and then a cross. Again, there is a good chance that my opponent will attempt to counter after I throw these two punches, so I will immediately pivot on my lead foot and circle around his body. Although this pivot takes me toward my opponent's power side, I throw a lead hook at the same time. If you look at the photos below, you'll notice that landing the hook turns his body away from me, making it very difficult for him to counter. Once accomplished, I am out of his line of fire and have a dominant angle of attack. This gives me the option of creating space between us or launching another attack.

1 Lance and I are in the same fighting stance, searching for an opening to attack.

2 Shifting my weight onto my rear leg, I pivot on the ball of my lead foot, rotate my hips in a clockwise direction, and throw a lead hook to the side of his head.

3 Shifting my weight onto my lead leg, I come up onto the ball of my rear foot, rotate my hips in a counterclockwise direction, and throw a right cross straight down the middle and into Lance's face.

4 Having landed two strikes, Lance will most likely counter. To avoid that counter, I pivot on the ball of my lead foot and slide my rear foot across the canvas in a clockwise direction. At the same time, I throw a lead hook to the side of his jaw. Notice how my hook turns his head toward his left side, making it difficult for him to square his hips with my hips and launch a counterattack.

5 After landing the lead hook, Lance begins rotating his body in a clockwise direction in an attempt to square his hips with my hips, which would allow him to launch a counterattack. To prepare myself, I pull my arm back into my stance and back away.

Forrest Griffin

Jab - Cross - Body Hook - Pivot - Cross

Like many combinations, I begin this one with the traditional jab/cross. Although it's great when I can land either of these punches, the primary reason for throwing them is to obstruct my opponent's vision and force him to elevate his arms to protect his head. This sets me up to deliver a powerful lead hook to his unprotected liver. As I mentioned in previous sequences, anytime you throw two or three punches in a row, there is a good chance that your opponent will attempt to dish out some payback. To avoid his counterstrikes, immediately after landing the hook I will elevate my hand to his near shoulder and push him in a counterclockwise direction. At the same time, I will pivot on my lead foot and circle around to the outside of his body. These actions move me out of the danger zone, square my hips with my opponent's, and turns my opponent's hips away from me. In order for him to launch an effective strike, he must first square his hips with mine. Before he can accomplish this, I conclude the combination with a cross.

Technical Note: If you look at the photos below, you'll notice that my first two punches actually strike my opponent's arms. Although this technically shouldn't score you any points in a fight, the majority of the time the judges can't tell exactly what you are hitting. As long as you can move your opponent's body or head, you will most likely rack up some points on the score cards.

Lance and I are in orthodox stances, searching for an opening to attack.

I throw a jab to Lance's head to force his focus and arms high.

I take an outward step with my lead foot, rotate my hips in a counterclockwise direction, come up onto the ball of my rear foot, and throw a cross at Lance's face. Notice how he has elevated both arms to protect his head.

With Lance focused on protecting his head, I rotate my body in a clockwise direction and deliver a lead hook to his liver.

Having landed three punches in a row, Lance will most likely counter. To hinder him from accomplishing this, I elevate my lead hand immediately after throwing the cross and place it on his right shoulder.

Pivoting on the ball of my lead foot, I slide my right foot in a clockwise direction across the mat. At the same time, I drive my left hand into Lance's shoulder, turning his body in a counterclockwise direction.

Having disrupted Lance's base, he rotates in a clockwise direction in order to square his hips with my hips.

Before Lance can square his hips with my hips and launch a counterattack, I throw a cross at his chin.

Shawn Tompkins

Jab - Cross - Body Hook - Hook - Cross

I begin this combination with the traditional jab/cross to get my opponent to elevate his guard to protect his face, and then I throw a powerful lead hook to his exposed liver. By rotating my hips into the body shot, I set myself up to immediately throw a rear-handed punch. However, instead of unleashing a rear-handed strike, I quickly reload my hips in the opposite direction to set myself up for another lead-handed strike. This serves two purposes. Anytime you land a lead hook to your opponent's body, there is a strong chance that he will immediately counter with a cross. By reloading your hips, you're executing the same movements involved in an outside slip, which moves your head away from your centerline. If your opponent does in fact counter with a cross, your face will be out of the way. Second, it breaks up your rhythm. When in a heated striking battle, your opponent will often get accustomed to your combinations. If you always throw a right hand after a left and a left hand after a right, he can prepare his defenses. By throwing two lead-handed strikes in a row, you become a lot more unpredictable, which dramatically increases your odds of landing your strikes successfully.

Junie and I are in orthodox stances, searching for an opening to attack.

I initiate action by throwing a jab to Junie's chin.

I pull my left arm back into my stance and begin rotating my hips in a counterclockwise direction.

Continuing to rotate in a counterclockwise direction, I come up onto the ball of my right foot and throw a cross at Junie's chin.

I execute an outside slip by dropping my left shoulder and moving my head toward my left side. Notice how this spring-loads my hips.

Shifting my weight onto my lead leg, I rotate my hips and shoulders in a clockwise direction and drop my left arm to throw a lead hook.

Still rotating my hips in a clockwise direction, I land a lead hook to Junie's liver.

With Junie now focused on protecting his body, I rotate my body in a counterclockwise direction to once again spring-load my hips.

I rotate my hips in a clockwise direction and throw a second lead hook, except this one is aimed at Junie's jaw.

I land a lead hook to Junie's jaw.

I pull my arm back into my stance and begin rotating my hips in a counterclockwise direction.

Coming up onto the ball of my right foot, I throw a right cross to Junie's chin.

Switch Stepping to Strikes

I begin this attack with what Peter Welsh, the boxing trainer on the first season of the Ultimate Fighter, calls a "wrong-stepping jab." Instead of stepping your lead foot forward and throwing the jab, you step your rear foot forward and to the outside of your opponent's body as you throw the jab. In addition to adding a whole lot of power to your jab, it also gives you a dominant angle of attack and allows you to immediately follow up with a cross. The majority of the time, your opponent will attempt to square his hips with your hips and launch a counterattack after you throw these first two punches, but to prevent him from landing, you again step your rear foot forward and to the outside of his body, putting you off to his side and out of his line of fire. At the same time, you throw a lead hook. Having landed three strikes in a row, you do what I call a "walk away." Already positioned off to his side, you place your rear foot in front of your lead foot, just as if you were taking a normal step. This moves you even further around to your opponent's backside. Clear of any possible counters, you conclude the combination by pivoting your body to once again square your hips with your opponent.

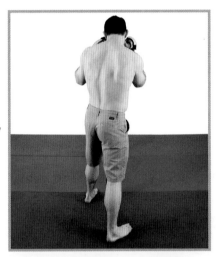

Lance and I are in orthodox stances, searching for an opening to attack.

To remove myself from Lance's line of fire and acquire a dominant angle of attack, I step my rear foot forward and to the outside of his lead leg. At the same time, I throw a jab. However, because I step my rear foot forward as I throw the punch, it packs as much power as a cross.

Having established a dominant angle of attack, I step my left foot forward, rotate my hips and shoulders in a counterclockwise direction, and throw another jab. Just as with the first punch, the punch packs a lot more power than the regular jab because I stepped my rear foot forward when throwing it.

I step my right foot forward and further to the outside of Lance's lead leg. Notice how this almost puts me on the same horizontal line as him. At the same time, I throw a lead hook. Just as with the previous two strikes, this punch packs more power because I stepped forward when throwing it.

In order to maintain my dominant angle of attack, I need to square my hips with Lance's hips. To begin this process, I step my left foot past my right foot and begin rotating my body in a counter-clockwise direction.

As my left foot touches down, I step my right foot forward and rotate my body so that I am once again square with my opponent.

Forrest Griffin

Stepping Jab - Shuffle Step - Lead Hook

Just like in the previous sequence, I begin this combination with a "wrong-stepping jab" to acquire a dominant angle of attack. However, instead of following up with a cross, I execute a "load step." To accomplish this, I skip my rear foot up to my lead foot and skip my lead foot behind my opponent's lead leg. During this transition, I also rotate my body, which primes my hips to throw a powerful lead hook. Once I've uncoiled my hips and landed the lead hook, I execute another load step to get further behind my opponent and avoid any counterattacks. While earlier in my career I found it entertaining to stand in the pocket and trade blows with my opponents, these days I would rather not get punched in the face if I can help it. If you have the same philosophy, this is an excellent technique because it allows you to quickly acquire a dominant angle of attack, land some strikes, and then get the hell out of dodge before your opponent can retaliate.

Lance and I are in orthodox stances, searching for an opening to attack. Notice how we are currently out of striking range.

To close the distance and acquire a dominant angle of attack, I step my right foot forward and to the outside of Lance's lead leg. At the same time, I throw a jab. Having switched my stance as I threw the punch, it is more powerful than a regular jab.

To establish an even more dominant angle, I begin rotating my body in a counterclockwise direction, shift my weight onto my right leg, and begin sliding my left foot toward my right foot.

4

I set my left foot down next to my right foot, shift my weight onto my left leg, and then skip my right foot further to the outside of Lance's lead leg (it is important to mention that this is done in one fluid motion). At the same time, I continue with my counterclockwise rotation. Notice how this spring-loads my hips.

5

With my hips spring-loaded, I shift my weight onto my right leg, rotate my hips in a clockwise direction, come up onto the ball of my left foot, and throw a lead hook into Lance's face.

6

Immediately after landing the hook, I rotate my body in a counterclockwise direction, slide my left foot up to my right foot, and then skip my right foot even further behind Lance's lead leg.

7

Continuing with my counterclockwise rotation, when my right foot touches down, my hips are spring-loaded to throw another strike. Notice how my hips are currently facing Lance, while his hips are facing away from me. This is an optimal position from which to attack.

Forrest Griffin

Opponent on the Run

I begin this sequence with a "wrong-stepping jab," just as I did in the last two combinations. As I land my punch, my opponent steps his rear leg backward in an attempt to evade my attack. Instead of letting him move out of striking range, I execute another wrong-stepping jab. Again, my opponent backs up to flee from my combinations, giving me an opportunity to execute a third wrong-stepping jab. The key to success with this technique is to step to the outside of your opponent's body rather than directly into him. This will put your head off to the side and make it difficult for him to hit you with counterstrikes. While it is possible to beat a retreating opponent across the ring using this technique, I don't recommend executing more than three wrong-stepping jabs in a row because eventually your opponent will catch on and pivot out to one side or the other. If your momentum is still moving forward when he does this, you could inadvertently give him a dominant angle of attack.

1

Lance and I are in orthodox stances, searching for an opening to attack.

2

To remove myself from Lance's line of fire and acquire a dominant angle of attack, I step my right foot forward and to the outside of his lead leg. At the same time, I throw a jab.

3

Getting hit with my powerful jab, Lance steps his rear foot behind to create distance. I immediately close that distance by stepping my left foot forward and throwing a jab.

Lance slides his lead foot back to create more distance, and again I close that distance off by stepping my right foot forward and to the outside of his lead leg. At the same time, I throw another jab.

Lance continues to retreat, and I continue to come forward by stepping my left foot to the front and throwing another jab.

I step forward again with another jab to keep Lance from reestablishing his base and balance. Although it is possible to hunt your opponent across the ring in this fashion, you must be mindful that your opponent could suddenly cut an angle. If you keep your momentum moving forward in such a scenario, he can acquire a dominant angle of attack.

Shawn Tompkins

Jab - Lead Hook - Cross

This combination begins with a jab, but the goal is not to throw this initial punch with all your might and knock your opponent out. As a matter of fact, it doesn't even matter if you hit him. Your primary mission with the jab is to force your opponent to reach his hands forward to block it. This exposes his chin and ears, creating a pathway for the lead hook. It can be a little tricky because again you are throwing two consecutive punches with the same arm, but it can be a devastating combination. The key to success is rotating your hips just like you would when executing an outside slip immediately after landing the jab. Not only does this remove your head from your centerline, making it difficult for your opponent to hit you with counterstrikes, but it also loads your hips to throw a powerful lead hook. If it is difficult to see your target after slipping your body to the outside, simply throw your lead hook over your opponent's shoulder. With his hands extended from parrying your initial punch, you will almost always land to the side of his face or jaw. Upon completing the lead hook, your opponent's arms will spread wide to protect the sides of his face and your hips will be primed to throw a straight cross right down the middle. It's a very crafty combination, especially when you are standing in an orthodox stance and your opponent is in a southpaw stance, or vice versa. Due to the positioning of your feet, his lead arm will be very close to your lead hand. When you throw the jab at such close range, your opponent will have little choice but to block it, which is the reaction that allows you to land the hook. If your opponent should block the jab and then step back, it doesn't matter. As long as you rotate and load your hips prior to throwing the lead hook, you will have the spring in your legs needed to leap forward. However, it is important to talk about the rhythm of this technique because not all three punches are thrown one after another. Due to the rotation of your hips, there will be a slight pause between the jab and the lead hook.

Junie and I are in orthodox stances, searching for an opening to attack.

I initiate by throwing a jab.

To spring-load my hips for a lead hook, I pull my left arm back into my stance, rotate my hips and shoulders in a counterclockwise direction, and come up onto the ball of my right foot.

I rotate my hips in a clockwise direction, pivot on the ball of my lead foot, and throw a lead hook to the side of Junie's face.

I rotate my hips in a counterclockwise direction, shift my weight onto my lead leg, come up onto the ball of my right foot, and throw a cross at Junie's chin.

Forrest Griffin

Jab - Round Kick

In this sequence I demonstrate how to set up a rear round kick using a jab. The goal is not to land the jab as hard as you can, but rather to pull your opponent's focus high and momentarily blind him. As he elevates his arms to better protect his head, you follow up with a round kick to the outside of his lead leg. When studying the photos below, it is important to notice that immediately after landing the jab I begin pulling my lead shoulder back and rotating my hips. This allows me to flow directly from the jab into the kick. If you pull your arm back into your stance, reset your base, and then throw the kick, your opponent will most likely see the strike coming and either get out of the way or utilize a block. It is also important to notice that as I throw the kick, I do not whip my rear arm behind me. Although a lot of fighters prefer to do this because it allows them to generate more power in their kick, I feel it leaves my face too vulnerable. Instead, I will shoot my rear hand forward as though I'm throwing a cross. It removes a little power from my kick, but it serves as an excellent blockade should my opponent decide to strike in the middle of my kick.

Lance and I are in orthodox stances, searching for an opening to attack.

I step my left foot forward and to the outside of Lance's rear leg. At the same time, I throw a jab to pull his focus upward and momentarily blind him.

As I pull my left hand back into my stance, I shift my weight onto my lead leg, rotate my hips in a counterclockwise direction, and shoot my right hand toward the right side of his head.

Shooting my right hand to the right side of Lance's head to stifle any punches he might throw, I whip my hips in a counterclockwise direction, pivot on the ball of my left foot, and whip my right shin into the outside of his lead leg.

As I pull my leg back into my stance, I keep both hands up to protect myself from counterstrikes.

Anuwat Kaewsamrit

Jab - Cross - Low Round Kick (option 1)

This is a very common combination in both Muay Thai and mixed martial arts. To begin, throw a jab and a cross at your opponent's head to pull his focus high and force him to lean backward. Next, pull your cross arm back into your stance, reset your base, and then immediately launch a rear round kick at the outside of your opponent's lead leg. It's possible to throw the round kick immediately after the cross, but with both strikes coming from the same side of your body, neither strike will be as powerful. If your goal is to damage your opponent rather than just score points, I recommend resetting your base after the cross.

My opponent and I are in orthodox stances, searching for an opening to attack.

I step my left foot forward and throw a jab at my opponent's chin.

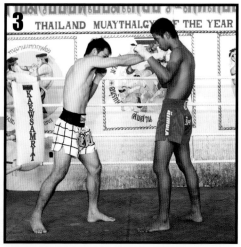

Rotating my hips in a counterclockwise direction, I come up onto the ball of my right foot and throw a cross at my opponent's chin.

I pull my right arm back and reestablish my fighting stance.

Once I have reacquired my base and balance, I take an outward step with my left foot, dip my head toward my left to avoid my opponent's cross, rotate my hips in a counterclockwise direction, and throw a rear round kick to the outside of my opponent's lead leg.

Remaining relaxed, I let the force of the impact push my right leg back into my fighting stance.

THE ULTIMATE MIXED MARTIAL ARTIST

PUNCH / KICK COMBINATIONS

Jab - Cross - Low Round Kick (option 2)

When you throw a jab into your opponent's face, he will usually react in one of three ways. He will either immediately launch a counterstrike, move backward to evade your punch, or elevate his arms to block the strike. If he chooses the last option, his arms will mostly likely impair part or all of his vision. In such a case, I like to step to the outside of his lead leg and then follow up with a cross to keep his guard elevated and his vision blocked. Once I have acquired a dominant angle, I conclude by throwing a rear low round kick to his lead hamstring. While this technique won't work with everyone, it is an excellent combo to employ against fighters who constantly block punches to avoid giving up ground, such as Tito Ortiz and Quinton Jackson.

Lance and I are in orthodox stances, searching for an opening to attack.

I step my lead foot forward and throw a jab at Lance's head to momentarily blind him and bring his focus high.

Upon landing the jab, I step my right foot forward and to the outside of Lance's lead leg. The instant my foot touches down, I slide my left foot toward my right foot, rotate my hips and shoulders in a counterclockwise direction, and throw a cross at the side of his head. Notice how by shifting off line I have created a dominant angle of attack.

I throw my right arm down to my right side, rotate my hips in a counterclockwise direction, pivot on the ball of my left foot, and throw a right round kick to the outside of Lance's lead leg. It is important to notice the positioning of my right hand. Normally I would throw my right hand in front of my opponent's arms to protect myself from his punches, but having moved off to his side, it isn't necessary. In this case, I throw my arm down to my side to generate more power in my kick.

I let the impact of my kick push my leg back into my fighting stance. Before Lance can square his hips with mine and launch a counterattack, I back away.

Anuwat Kaewsamrit

Jab - Cross - Jab - Low Kick

Although the jab to cross to low Thai kick I demonstrated earlier is an excellent combination, after using it a couple of times in a fight, my opponent will usually catch on and check the kick. To switch things up and keep him guessing, I'll throw a jab, a cross, another jab, and a low Thai kick. The nice part about this combo is that there is no need to reset your stance between the final jab and the kick. With your hips already spring-loaded from the jab, you can flow directly into the low kick.

My opponent and I are in orthodox stances, searching for an opening to attack.

I step my left foot forward and throw a jab at my opponent's chin.

As I pull my left hand back, I rotate my hips in a counterclockwise direction, come up onto the ball of my right foot, and throw a cross at my opponent's chin.

As I pull my right arm back, I rotate my hips in a clockwise direction and throw a second jab at my opponent's chin.

As I pull my left arm back into my stance, I rotate my hips in a counterclockwise direction, lean toward my left side to avoid my opponent's punches, pivot on the ball of my left foot, and throw a right round kick to the outside of his lead leg.

Anuwat Kaewsamrit

Jab - Cross - Uppercut - Low Round Kick

This is another combination that I will frequently utilize to keep my opponent guessing. Just as with the previous combo, it begins with a jab and a cross, but instead of following up with a low Thai kick or another jab, I will unleash a lead uppercut to lift my opponent's head. As his weight is forced onto his back leg, I conclude with a rear low kick to his lead leg. It is important to mention that this technique is not better or worse than the previous one—it's simply another option. The more options you learn, the harder it becomes for your opponent to figure you out and stifle your attacks.

My opponent and I are in orthodox stances, searching for an opening to attack.

I step my left foot forward and throw a jab at my opponent's chin.

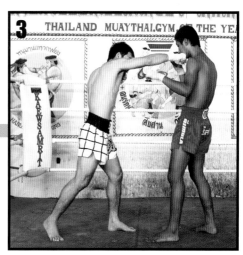

As I pull my left arm back, I rotate my hips in a counterclockwise direction, come up onto the ball of my right foot, and throw a cross at my opponent's chin.

As I pull my right arm back into my stance, I rotate my hips in a clockwise direction, lean slightly forward, and throw a lead uppercut to my opponent's chin.

The instant my uppercut lands, I begin rotating my hips in a counterclockwise direction.

Continuing with my rotation, I pivot on the ball of my left foot, dip my head toward my left to avoid my opponent's punches, and throw a right round kick to the outside of his lead leg.

Shawn Tompkins

Cross - Hook - Low Round Kick

This combination can be used either offensively or defensively. To employ it as an attack, step forward on the cross to cover the distance and then immediately follow up with a lead hook. However, instead of turning your hook over so that your palm is facing the ground, keep your palm facing toward you. As mentioned earlier in the book, this type of hook doesn't possess as much snap, but it has a lot more pushing power, which is what you desire in this particular combination. The goal is to move your opponent's body to the side with the hook, causing him to plant the majority of his weight onto his lead leg. Not only does this make it more difficult for him to lift his lead leg and block your rear round kick, but it also makes his leg tight, which allows you to cause his quadriceps more damage with your shin. The best time to use this combo defensively is when you're up against an opponent who constantly presses forward. With your opponent already moving toward you, there is no need to step into the cross. Just throw it directly from your stance. Once it lands, sit your weight onto your back leg and throw the lead hook. Again, the hook will move your opponent to the side, setting you up to land a kick to his leg. However, it is important to mention that when you land a powerful leg kick, your opponent's natural reaction will most likely be to immediately throw a leg kick of his own. To avoid his shot, immediately circle to the outside of your opponent's body upon completing your combination.

Junie and I are in orthodox stances, searching for an opening to attack.

I step my left foot forward and to the outside of Junie's rear leg.

Rotating my hips in a counterclockwise direction, I come up onto the ball of my right foot and throw a cross at Junie's chin.

Shifting my weight onto my rear leg, I rotate my hips in a clockwise direction and throw a lead hook toward the right side of Junie's jaw.

Pivoting on the ball of my left foot, I strike Junie's jaw with a left hook.

As I pull my left arm back into my stance, I rotate my hips in a counterclockwise direction.

Continuing with my counterclockwise rotation, I pivot on the ball of my left foot and throw a rear round kick toward the outside of Junie's lead leg. Notice how I elevate my leg above his thigh, which allows me to chop my kick down into his muscle.

Turning my hips over, I slice my kick downward into the outside of Junie's lead leg.

I let the force of the impact push my right leg back into my fighting stance.

Shawn Tompkins

Jab - Cross to Body - Hook - Low Round Kick

This is a very crafty combination because in addition to alternating your strikes from high to low, you also change your levels, which will often confuse your opponent. To begin, throw a jab at your opponent's face. This will often cause him to lean back in defense, making his entire midsection vulnerable. To capitalize on that vulnerability, drop your level and throw a powerful cross to his sternum. When you land clean, the power from your shot will fold your opponent forward and cause him to drop his hands to guard his body. The instant this occurs, increase your elevation and throw a lead hook to the side of his head. As you already learned, landing the hook moves your opponent to the side and causes him to plant his weight on his lead leg, allowing you to cause damage with a powerful rear low kick to his leg.

While it is possible to throw all of your strikes in this combination from an upright position, I strongly suggest dropping your level for the cross because it plays mind games with your opponent. Uncertain whether you are about to throw a punch or shoot in for a takedown, his focus divides, which in turn weakens his defenses. It is important to note that the last strike in this combination doesn't have to be a low kick. Personally, I like the low kick because it disrupts my opponent's balance and allows me a moment to escape his line of fire, but if you are a wrestler and want to take your opponent to the mat, you can just as easily shoot in for a takedown.

1

Junie and I are in orthodox stances, searching for an opening to attack.

2

Shifting my weight onto my lead leg, I throw a jab at Junie's face.

3

Immediately after landing the jab, I drop my elevation by bending at the knees. Notice how I have not leaned forward.

4

Maintaining my low stance, I rotate my hips in a counterclockwise direction and throw a cross at Junie's sternum.

5

As I pull my right arm back into my stance, I plant my right foot on the mat, shift my weight onto my right leg, come up onto the ball of my left foot, and begin rotating my hips in a clockwise direction.

6

Continuing with my clockwise rotation, I throw a left hook at the side of Junie's face.

7

As I pull my left arm back into my stance, I step my left foot forward and further to the outside of Junie's rear leg. This not only sets me up for a more powerful kick, but it also removes my head from his line of fire.

8

Rotating my hips in a counterclockwise direction, I pivot on the ball of my left foot and throw a right rear round kick to the outside of Junie's lead leg.

Shawn Tompkins

Jab - Cross - Outside Step - Low Round Kick

This combination is called the two-outside-run. It's not a very complex combination, but timing is very important. The goal is to throw a very powerful jab-cross at your opponent to bait him into leaning forward and throwing a retaliatory punch. Instead of letting him hit you with that strike, you step to the outside of his lead leg and remove yourself from his line of fire, causing him to miss. While his arm is still outstretched, you throw a rear round kick to the outside of his lead leg. With the majority of his weight now positioned over that leg due to his strike, it knocks him off balance and does serious damage to his tendons.

Before Chris Horodecki fought Ryan Schultz in the IFL, he trained this technique tirelessly. We knew Schultz was an amazing wrestler and would be looking for a takedown. We also knew that when an opponent hit him with punches, he tended to retaliate with a big, looping overhand. This particular combination was an excellent answer to both attacks. By throwing two punches and stepping to the outside, Horodecki would avoid the looping overhand, and by following up with the low leg kick, he would damage Schultz's lead leg, making it more difficult for him to shoot in for a takedown as the fight progressed. Come fight night, it worked out perfectly. After abusing Schultz's lead leg with this combination, Schultz began shooting in for the takedown, but his shots were slow and awkward because he was unable to put any weight on his damaged leg. As a result, Horodecki was able to keep the fight standing and knock Schultz out with a kick to the head.

The key to success with this technique is with the outside run. Instead of simply stepping your rear foot to the outside of your opponent's lead leg, you also want to slide your lead foot to the outside of his lead leg. This gives you a very dominant angle of attack and allows you to soccer kick the back of your opponent's leg, causing the most damage possible. It is also important to note that if your goal is to take the fight to the ground, you can pass on the leg kick and secure a body lock instead. Due to your dramatic angle, you'll usually be in a prime position to lift your opponent off the mat and execute a belly-to-back suplex.

1

Junie and I are in orthodox stances, searching for an opening to attack.

2

I shift my weight onto my lead leg and throw a jab at Junie's chin.

3

As I pull my left arm back into my stance, I rotate my hips in a counterclockwise direction and come up onto the ball of my right foot.

Continuing to rotate in a counterclockwise direction, I throw a cross at Junie's chin.

I pull my right arm back into my stance.

I step my right foot to the outside of Junie's lead leg and then begin sliding my left foot in the same direction.

Once I have slid my left foot to the outside of Junie's lead leg, I rotate my hips in a counterclockwise direction.

Continuing to rotate my hips in a counterclockwise direction, I pivot on the ball of my left foot and whip my right leg toward the outside of Junie's left leg.

Still pivoting on the ball of my left foot, I kick the back of Junie's left leg.

Forrest Griffin

Jab - Low Round Kick - Lead Hook - Low Round Kick

This is an excellent combination that I feel is largely overlooked. It starts with the basic jab and then low Thai kick to the outside of your opponent's lead leg, but instead of simply pulling your leg back into your stance as most fighters do, you throw a lead hook at the same time. It's not a hard strike to master because when you pull your leg back into your stance, the movement of your body generates all the force you need to deliver a powerful lead hook. It's also deceiving because with just one foot planted on the mat, your opponent will most likely see you as vulnerable. A lot of times he will come forward as you retract your kick to launch an attack of his own, which causes him to walk straight into your lead hook. Once you land the hook, it will most likely push your opponent off balance. This not only makes it difficult for him to launch a counterstrike, but it also opens you up to throw another low kick to the outside of his lead leg. When studying the photos, it is important to notice that I extend my rear arm across my opponent's body as I throw the initial kick. Although throwing your arm behind you is typical and allows you to generate more force behind your kick, it leaves you vulnerable to your opponent's cross. Having eaten many crosses in my day, trust me when I say this is the preferred method. It is also important to notice that immediately after landing the second kick, I pivot on my lead foot and circle around to the outside of my opponent's body to avoid his possible counters.

Lance and I are in orthodox stances, searching for an opening to attack.

I step my left foot forward and throw a jab at Lance's face.

As I pull my left arm back into my stance, I come up onto the ball of my left foot and begin rotating my hips in a counterclockwise direction.

Continuing to rotate my hips in a counterclockwise direction, I pivot on the ball of my left foot, throw my right arm toward the right side of Lance's head to hinder him from countering with punches, and throw a right round kick to the outside of his lead leg.

PUNCH / KICK COMBINATIONS

THE ULTIMATE MIXED MARTIAL ARTIST

As I let the force of the impact pull my right leg back into my stance, I rotate my hips in a clockwise direction and throw a lead hook.

Still rotating my hips in a clockwise direction, I shift my weight onto my right leg, pivot on the ball of my left foot, and land a left hook to the side of Lance's face.

As I pull my left arm back into my stance, I step my left foot forward and to the outside of Lance's rear leg.

Rotating my hips in a counterclockwise direction, I throw my right arm down to my right side to generate power in my strike and throw a right round kick to the outside of Lance's lead leg. It is important to mention that had I remained in front of Lance, I would have thrown my right arm across his body to hinder him from countering my kick with punches.

I let the impact of the kick whip my leg back into my fighting stance. Notice how my hips are now square with Lance's hips, giving me a dominant angle of attack. In order to eliminate that dominant angle, he must first square his hips with mine.

Forrest Griffin

Step-Out / Step-In Low Kick / Hook

This is one of my bread-and-butter combinations. I'll sometimes use it as a straight-up attack, but most of the time I will employ it to finish up another combination, especially if I see that my opponent is hurt. If you look at the photos below, you'll notice that I begin in the pocket, which means my opponent has just as good a chance of hitting me as I do of hitting him. To shake things up, I will hop to the outside of my opponent's lead leg, giving me a dominant angle of attack. As my opponent turns to face me, I'll leap back into him and deliver a rear low kick to the outside of his lead leg. The impact of the blow turns his hips further away from me, buying me another split second before he can square his hips with mine. In this interim, I follow up with a hook to the center of his face. The key to success with this combination is not committing to it too early. If you hop to the outside of your opponent's lead leg and he quickly squares up with you, hopping back into him might allow him to land a powerful cross to your face. In such a situation, abandon the combination and circle out. When fighting, it is important to have the mentality of a baseball pitcher. If you don't like what you see, shake it off and move on to something else.

Lance and I are in orthodox stances, searching for an opening to attack.

Instead of attacking Lance straight on, I shoot my right foot forward and to the outside of his body. The instant my foot touches down, I slide my left foot toward my right so that it too is positioned to the outside of his lead leg.

Shifting my weight onto my left foot, I rotate my hips in a counterclockwise direction, pivot on the ball of my left foot, and throw a right round kick into the outside of Lance's lead leg. Having removed myself from his line of fire, I throw my right hand down to my right side to generate more power in my kick.

As the impact of my kick whips my right leg back into my stance, I rotate my hips in a clockwise direction, pivot on the ball of my left foot, and throw a lead hook into Lance's face.

Shawn Tompkins

Cross - Mid Round Kick - Cross

In this sequence my opponent and I are in opposite fighting stances, and I unleash with a powerful three-strike combination. It's not the fastest combination because all three strikes come from one side of your body, which requires you to reset your hips between each strike, but when your opponent is wounded or backed up against the fence, it is an excellent combination for inflicting serious damage. Just like previous combos, this one follows the low/high principle. It begins with a cross to your opponent's face to pull his focus high, followed by a rear round kick into his midsection to force him to bend over and drop his focus low, and then you go high again with a second cross.

Junie is in a southpaw stance, and I'm in an orthodox stance. Both of us are searching for an opening to attack.

I shift my weight onto my lead leg, come up onto the ball of my right foot, rotate my hips in a counterclockwise direction, and throw a right cross at Junie's face.

I pull my right arm back and reestablish my fighting stance.

Once I have my base and balance, I rotate my hips in a counterclockwise direction, pivot on the ball of my left foot, and throw a right round kick to Junie's midsection.

I let the force of the blow push my right leg back into my fighting stance.

Once I have reestablished my base and balance, I shift my weight onto my lead leg, rotate my hips in a counterclockwise direction, come up onto the ball of my right foot, and throw a cross at Junie's chin.

Shawn Tompkins

Jab - Switch Step - Mid Round Kick

This is a combination that my fighter Sam Stout uses in most of his fights. The goal is to throw a jab to get your opponent to cover high and lean back, which in turns exposes the ribs on both sides of his body. While it's quite possible to follow up with a rear round kick to his kidney, it's an easy kick for your opponent to catch. And if he does catch your kick, it can be a difficult position to escape because your opponent has control of your power leg. To avoid this possible outcome, instead of following the jab with a rear round kick, execute a switch step and throw a lead round kick to your opponent's liver. Not only is it a more difficult kick for your opponent to catch due to the positioning of your bodies, but if he should catch your kick, it's also a lot easier to free your leg. All you have to do is rotate your body away from him and pull your leg out of his grasp.

Junie and I are in orthodox stances, searching for an opening to attack.

I shift my weight onto my lead leg and throw a jab at Junie's chin.

I pull my left arm back toward my body and redistribute my weight onto both legs.

I hop up into the air and reverse the positioning of my feet.

I land with my right foot forward and my left foot back

Rotating my hips in a clockwise direction, I pivot on the ball of my right foot and throw a left round kick to Junie's liver.

Shawn Tompkins

Cross - Inside Lead-Leg Kick - Cross

In this combination, each strike spring-loads your hips for the strike to follow. Standing in the same fighting stance as your opponent, you lead with a powerful cross to your opponent's chin. This forces him to lean his head back, which in turn removes his weight from his lead leg. Immediately rotating your hips in the opposite direction, you throw a lead round kick to the inside of his lead leg. However, you do not want to throw a snappy kick, but rather drive your shin into his inner thigh to lift his leg off the ground. With your opponent now balanced on one leg and his chin floating, you rotate your hips in the opposite direction and conclude with another cross.

I know for a fact this particular combination can be successful in the top-tier of MMA because Randy Couture used it against Tim Sylvia. Going into the fight, we knew that Randy was outmatched in the boxing department. If he attempted to straight-up box with Sylvia, he would most likely lose. To level the playing field, we had Randy leading with powerful crosses and then immediately following up with inside leg kicks. The inside leg kicks threw Sylvia off balance, which achieved several goals—it made it very difficult for him to counter Randy's punches, it lifted his chin, and it created an avenue for Randy to throw yet another power punch. When Randy dropped Tim in the first round using this combo, I wasn't surprised in the least.

Junie and I are in orthodox stances, searching for an opening to attack.

Rotating my hips in a counterclockwise direction, I come up onto the ball of my right foot and throw a cross at Junie's chin.

As I pull my right arm back into my stance, I shift my weight toward my back leg and begin rotating my hips in a clockwise direction.

With my weight now on my back leg, I rotate my hips in a clockwise direction, pivot on the ball of my right foot, and throw a kick to the inside of Junie's lead leg, lifting it off the mat.

Having disrupted Junie's base and balance with my inside leg kick, I pull my left leg back into my stance and begin rotating my hips in a counterclockwise direction.

Still rotating my hips in a counterclockwise direction, I plant my left foot on the mat, come up onto the ball of my right foot, and throw a cross at Junie's chin.

Anuwat Kaewsamrit

Front Kick - Round Kick - Push - Round Kick

This combination begins with a push kick, which is a lot like a jab. It doesn't cause a lot of damage, but it's a very fast and distracting strike that can knock your opponent backward and disrupt his balance. In this particular combination, I target my opponent's lead hip with the push kick to collapse his body forward and force his weight onto his lead leg. Once accomplished, I immediately follow up with a rear Thai kick to his ribs. Instead of flowing directly into another strike, I pull my leg back into my stance and reestablish my base. As I mentioned earlier in the book, whenever you throw a kick, your opponent will most likely instinctively throw the exact same kick right back. To prevent him from landing that kick, I step directly into him, place my hand on his chest, and shove him backward. As he attempts to regain his base, I'll conclude the combination by throwing another rear Thai kick to his midsection. The only time I won't use this technique is when I'm up against an opponent who is primarily a puncher because instead of countering my initial kick with a kick of his own, he will most likely instinctively counter with a linear punch. As you can image, stepping into a cross is not a lot of fun.

My opponent and I are in orthodox stances, searching for an opening to attack.

Shifting my weight onto my right leg, I elevate my left leg and throw a push kick to my opponent's lead hip to disrupt his base and balance.

I pull my left leg back toward my body and then step my foot down to the canvas. Notice how my left foot is angled toward my left side at a forty-five-degree angle. This makes for a smoother transition into the round kick.

Rotating my hips in a counterclockwise direction, I pivot on the ball of my left foot and throw a right round kick to my opponent's ribs.

I let the impact of my kick push my leg back into my fighting stance.

I step my right foot forward to cover the distance.

I step my left foot forward and place my left hand on my opponent's chest.

I push my opponent backward to disrupt his base and balance.

Rotating my hips in a counterclockwise direction, I pivot on the ball of my left foot, throw my right arm behind me to generate power, and land a right round kick to my opponent's ribs.

Forrest Griffin

PUNCH / KICK COMBINATIONS

Outside Pivot - Hook - Round Kick to Body - Hook

In earlier sequences I demonstrated how to launch a linear attack and then conclude the combination by throwing a lead hook and pivoting to the outside of your opponent's body to acquire a dominant angle of attack and evade your opponent's counterstrikes. This combination is slightly different because you begin with a lead hook and outside pivot, which comes in handy when up against an opponent who is an aggressive counterstriker. In addition to removing your body and head from his line of fire, it also sets you up perfectly for a rear round kick to his midsection. After you land the kick, your opponent will most likely attempt to square his hips with your hips and launch a counterattack. To prevent that from happening, you throw a second lead hook as you pull your leg back into your stance, once again disrupting his base and balance.

Lance and I are in orthodox stances, searching for an opening to attack.

I step my left foot forward and to the outside of Lance's rear leg to acquire a dominant angle of attack. At the same time, I begin rotating my hips in a clockwise direction and throwing a lead hook.

Pivoting on the ball of my left foot, I slide my right foot in a clockwise direction along the canvas and land a lead hook to the side of Lance's face.

Having established a very dominant angle of attack, I rotate my hips in a counterclockwise direction, pivot on the ball of my left foot, throw my right arm behind me, and land a right round kick to Lance's midsection.

As the impact of my kick pushes my leg back into my fighting stance, I rotate my hips in a clockwise direction and throw another lead hook

Continuing with my clockwise rotation, I come up onto the ball of my left foot and land a hook to the side of Lance's face.

Advancing Combo to Kick

I begin this combination with a "wrong-step jab," just as I did in earlier techniques. With it being a very powerful punch, chances are you will either push your opponent backward with your fist or he will step backward to avoid the blow. To stay within striking range and remain on the attack, I follow up with two more "wrong-step jabs," each one pushing my opponent further back. If you catch your opponent off guard with your initial strike, a lot of the time he will begin a rapid retreat in an attempt to evade your barrage. Instead of reaching for my opponent's head as he falls out of punching range, I will conclude the combination with a round kick to his head. I utilized this combination somewhat effectively when I fought Quinton Jackson. Of course, I missed the head kick by a mile, but at least I landed the punches.

Lance and I are in orthodox stances, searching for an opening to attack.

As I step my right foot forward and to the outside of Lance's lead leg, I throw a jab at his chin.

As Lance backs up in an attempt to avoid my strikes, I step my left foot in front of my right foot, rotate my hips and shoulders in a counterclockwise direction, and throw another jab at his face.

I keep Lance on the run by stepping my right foot forward and to the outside of his right leg and throwing another jab.

Having pushed Lance back with my strikes and disrupted his balance, I step my left foot forward, rotate my hips in a counterclockwise direction, and throw a right round kick at his head.

Shawn Tompkins

Jab - Inside Lead Low Kick - Cross

If you look at the photos in the sequence below, you'll notice that this combination is utilized when you and your opponent are in opposite fighting stances. It's a three-strike combo, but the first two strikes are mere setups for the final blow, which is a powerful cross. To begin, throw a jab at your opponent's chin. The goal is not to cause a lot of damage with the strike, but rather force your opponent to lean backward, making his lead leg vulnerable. It's simply a way to open the door. Next, throw a rear round kick to the inside of his lead leg. For the best results, drive your shin into the flesh of his inner thigh hard enough to lift his leg off the mat. This creates what I often refer to as "chin float." With your opponent now balanced on one leg, his chin floats in the air and becomes vulnerable. To capitalize on that vulnerability, conclude the combination with a powerful cross. The most difficult part of this technique to master is throwing the cross immediately after the kick because they are both thrown from the same side of your body. In order to generate power in the cross, you must first pull your kicking leg back into your stance and load your hips. The more fluid you become at reacquiring your balance off your kick, the more success you will have with this combination.

Junie is in a southpaw stance, and I am in an orthodox stance. Both of us are searching for an opening to attack.	**I shift my weight onto my left leg and throw a jab at Junie's face.**	**I pull my left arm back and reestablish my fighting stance.**

I angle my left foot toward the outside of my body at a forty-five-degree angle. At the same time, I begin rotating my hips in a counterclockwise direction.

Pivoting on the ball of my left foot, I throw a round kick to the inside of Junie's lead leg, lifting it off the mat.

I elevate Junie's right leg as high as possible to disrupt his base and balance.

I pull my right leg back into my fighting stance and reestablish my base.

While Junie is still trying to reestablish his stance, I rotate my hips in a counterclockwise direction, come up onto the ball of my right foot, and throw a cross at his chin.

Shawn Tompkins

Jab - Cross - Inside Kick - Cross - Hook - Kick

Although this is an elaborate combination, it is fairly easy to execute because you use the momentum from one strike to flow directly into the next. The goal here is to overwhelm your opponent with not only straight and looping punches, but also strikes that target both his upper and lower body. In an actual fight it might be difficult to unleash so many strikes in a row without your opponent countering, but practicing combos like this one will help perfect your hip rotation.

Junie and I are in orthodox stances, searching for an opening to attack.

I shift my weight onto my left leg and throw a jab at Junie's face.

As I pull my left arm back, I begin rotating my hips in a counterclockwise direction and come up onto the ball of my right foot.

Continuing to rotate in a counterclockwise direction, I throw a right cross at Junie's chin.

I pull my right arm back and reestablish my fighting stance.

I slide my right foot up to my left foot.

Shifting my weight onto my right leg, I throw a left round kick at the inside of Junie's left leg, lifting it off the mat.

I let the impact of my kick push my leg back into my fighting stance.

While Junie is still attempting to reestablish his balance, I rotate my hips in a counterclockwise direction, come up onto the ball of my right foot, and throw a cross.

As I pull my right arm back into my stance, I shift my weight onto my back leg, rotate my body in a clockwise direction, and throw a left hook toward the right side of Junie's face.

Continuing to rotate my hips in a clockwise direction, I land a lead hook to the right side of Junie's jaw.

As I pull my left arm back into my stance, I begin sliding my left foot to the outside of Junie's rear leg. In addition to giving me a dominant angle of attack, it also removes me from his line of fire.

Planting my left foot to the outside of Junie's right leg, I rotate my hips in a counterclockwise direction, pivot on the ball of my left foot, and throw a right round kick toward the outside of his lead leg.

Turing my hips over, I crash my right shin down into the outside of Junie's right leg.

I let the impact of my kick push my leg back into my fighting stance.

Forrest Griffin

Cross - Outside Step - Inside Kick - Low Kick

This sequence begins with a cross, and as I mentioned earlier, your opponent will usually react to the cross in one of two ways— either he will move backward to evade the strike or he will elevate his arm to block it. If he chooses the later, chances are he will immediately attempt to counter with a cross of his own. To evade his punch and acquire a dominant angle of attack, the instant I land the cross I'll step my rear foot forward and to the outside of his lead leg. In addition to removing me from his line of fire, it also sets me up to throw a kick to the inside of his lead leg. A lot of times the combination will end here. Having disrupted my opponent's base and acquired a dominant angle of attack, I'll assess the situation and decide whether to back away or continue with more strikes. However, in some cases your opponent will instinctively throw a rear round kick immediately after you land the inside leg kick. In such a situation, I like to use my dominant angle to throw a rear round kick to the outside of his lead leg as his kick comes at me. When timed correctly, you sweep his grounded leg out from under him, putting him on his back.

Lance and I are in orthodox stances, searching for an opening to attack.

Rotating my hips in a counterclockwise direction, I come up onto the ball of my right foot and throw a cross at Lance's face.

While lance is still covered up, I step my right foot forward and to the outside of his lead leg.

I throw a left round kick to the inside of Lance's lead leg.

I let the impact of the kick push my leg back into my fighting stance.

Lance attempts to throw a rear round kick to the outside of my left leg. However, with my hips facing his body and his hips facing away from my body, I currently have the dominant angle of attack.

As Lance throws his kick, I rotate my hips in a counterclockwise direction, pivot on the ball of my left foot, and throw a right round kick to the outside of his left leg, zapping all power from his kick and most likely disrupting his balance.

Shawn Yarborough

Jab - Inside Leg Kick - Cross - Hook - Low Round Kick

I begin this sequence by throwing a jab to momentarily blind my opponent and force him to shift his weight onto his rear leg. This sets me up to throw a left round kick to the inside of his lead leg, further disrupting his balance. While he is trying to re-establish his base, I follow up with a cross and then a lead hook to his jaw. With my opponent thoroughly discombobulated, I finish the combo by stepping to the outside of his rear leg and throwing a rear low round kick.

Lance and I are in orthodox stances, searching for an opening to attack.

I throw a jab at Lance's face to distract him.

I slide my right foot up to my left foot.

I throw a left kick to the inside of Lance's lead leg, disrupting his balance and pulling his focus low.

I let the impact of my kick push my left leg back into my stance and then immediately rotate my hips in a counterclockwise direction and throw a cross.

I shift my weight onto my right leg, pivot on the ball of my left foot, and throw a left hook.

I land a left hook to Lance's jaw.

I step my left foot to the outside of Lance's rear leg and rotate my hips in a counterclockwise direction.

I throw my right hand out to hinder Lance from punching and deliver a right round kick to the outside of his left leg.

Forrest Griffin

Jab-Low Kick-Superman Punch

In this sequence I throw a jab and then immediately follow up with a rear round kick to the outside of my opponent's lead leg. The goal of the jab is to get him to lean backward, and the goal of the leg kick is to force his focus low and get him to fear my leg kicks. After landing the two strikes, I back away from my opponent to evade any possible counterstrikes. Next, I elevate my rear foot off the mat and throw my leg forward, just as I would when executing a rear round low kick. Having just eaten one such kick, my opponent's focus returns to his legs. However, instead of throwing the low kick, I quickly shoot my extended leg behind me, leap off the mat, and throw a superman punch at the side of his head. It's a very risky strike because both of your feet leave the mat, which eliminates your defenses. Luckily, leading with the jab/cross reduces much of that risk. With the jab having forced your opponent to lean backward, it becomes much harder for him to throw strikes. And fearful of absorbing another leg kick, he will most likely focus on defense rather than offense. The one thing you don't want to do is throw the superman punch naked (and by naked I mean not setting it up). With everyone and their mother now using the superman punch, it's no longer considered a crafty technique. If you fail to set it up, your opponent will most likely counter while you're in the air and ruin your day. It is also important not to commit to the reverse superman punch until the last second. If your opponent makes no movements to guard against the low kick, follow through with it.

Lance and I are in orthodox stances, searching for an opening to attack.

I step my left foot forward and throw a jab at Lance's face to distract him and pull his focus high.

As I pull my left arm back, I rotate my hips in a counterclockwise direction, pivot on the ball of my left foot, and throw a right round kick to the outside of Lance's lead leg.

I let the impact of my kick push my leg back into my fighting stance.

I throw my right leg forward as though I am about to throw another round kick.

As Lance drops his focus low, I shoot my right leg behind, leap upward off my left leg, rotate my hips in a counterclockwise direction, and throw a superman punch to Lance's jaw.

Blocked Superman Punch to Knee

In this sequence you throw a superman punch just like in the last, but your opponent spots the punch coming and blocks it with his lead arm. This can be a dangerous situation because he has remained in striking range, which makes it much easier for him to counter with strikes of his own. However, one nice attribute about the reverse superman punch is that it places your body to the outside of your opponent's lead leg. In order to throw strikes, he must first square his hips up with your hips. To prevent him from accomplishing this, shoot your rear hand forward off your failed punch, just as you would when throwing a cross, but instead of striking him in the head (which would do little good because he still has his blocking arm elevated), place your hand on the side of his head to prevent him from turning into you. Not only does this buy you time to regain your base and balance, but it also allows you to set up a powerful rear knee to his midsection.

Lance and I are in orthodox stances, searching for an opening to attack.

I throw my right leg forward as though I am about to execute a round kick. This forces Lance to drop his focus to the lower portion of his body.

Instead of following through with the kick, I shoot my right leg behind me, leap off the mat using my left foot, and throw a superman punch at the side of Lance's head. However, having spotted the punch coming, Lance elevates his lead arm in defense.

Immediately after my left foot touches down, I step my right foot forward to remain in striking range.

I shoot my left hand forward as though I am throwing a cross. However, instead of striking Lance in the head with my fist, I place my left hand on the side of his head and push him away to disrupt his balance. At the same time, I throw a left knee toward his midsection.

Keeping Lance off balance using my left hand, I drive my left knee into his midsection.

Forrest Griffin

Failed Superman Punch to Head Kick

As I already mentioned, the superman punch is becoming more common in MMA competition. If your opponent spots it coming, he will usually react in one of two ways. He will either block the strike, which allows you to throw the knee, or he will move backward to evade the powerful blow. If he choses the latter, you will most likely miss your strike. This is far from optimal because usually you'll land in a somewhat awkward position, but to make the best of the situation, I like to use the forward momentum of the punch to transition right into a head kick. The nice part about this combination is that a lot of fighters have a tendency to drop their hands as they back out of punching range, allowing you to land your kick clean. The most important part about this technique is to not stop after missing your first strike. When I was playing football, I used to go the wrong direction in drills. When I realized I had gone the wrong direction, I would just stop. The coach got furious at this, and he would tell me, "When you screw up, screw up a 100 percent. Don't stop in the middle—that is the worst thing that you can do." This particular combo can be a little risky because your opponent can always counter the kick with a cross, but it is a whole lot better than just standing there off balance after your failed superman punch.

Lance and I are in orthodox stances, searching for an opening to attack.

I fake a low round kick by throwing my right leg forward.

I attempt to land the superman punch by shooting my right leg behind me, leaping off the mat using my left foot, and throwing my right hand toward Lance's face. However, he spots the superman punch coming and leans back to avoid it.

Having missed my punch, I land in somewhat of an awkward position.

To make the best of a bad situation, I rotate my hips in a clockwise direction, pivot on the ball of my right foot, and throw a left round kick at the right side of Lance's head.

Anuwat Kaewsamrit

Jab - Cross - Knee - Push - Kick

In this sequence I utilize the traditional jab/cross to set up a powerful knee strike to my opponent's midsection. The jab and cross force him to lean back and distribute his weight onto his hind leg, and as he brings his weight forward to launch a counterattack, I step my rear foot forward and throw a knee strike to his abdomen. This puts us in punching range. Instead of pulling my leg back into my stance, which would make me vulnerable to my opponent's punches, I drop it straight down to the mat, place my lead hand on my opponent's chest, and push him away from me to create distance and again disrupt his balance. Before he can reestablish his stance, I conclude the combination with a rear Thai kick to his midsection. When studying the photos it is important to notice that during the combination I switch my stance twice. The first switch comes immediately after the cross, which sets me up to throw a powerful knee. The second switch comes immediately after the knee, which sets me up for the round kick.

My opponent and I are in orthodox stances. I throw a jab to initiate the action.

As I pull my left arm back, I rotate my hips in a counterclockwise direction, come up onto the ball of my right foot, and throw a cross at my opponent's chin.

Keeping my right arm extended to maintain distance, I step my right foot forward.

As I deliver a straight left knee to my opponent's midsection, I begin moving my left hand toward his chest.

As I drop my left foot back to the canvas, I push on my opponent's chest using my left hand to create separation and disrupt his balance.

Rotating my hips in a counterclockwise direction, I pivot on the ball of my left foot and throw a right round kick to my opponent's ribs.

Shawn Tompkins

Cross - Rear Elbow - Cross

This combination is a lot like the cross to rear round kick to cross combo demonstrated earlier in that it's an aggressive and powerful attack. Instead of throwing a rear-handed strike and then uncoiling your hips to flow directly into a lead-handed strike, you throw three rear-handed strikes in a row. Although this is considerably slower because you have to reestablish your fighting stance after each strike, it allows you to overwhelm your opponent with powerful strikes. To begin, throw a powerful cross. While you're pulling your arm back into your stance, monitor your opponent's reactions. If he is dazed and comes forward to tie you up in the clinch, unleash a powerful rear elbow to the side of his jaw. As you pull your elbow back into your stance, again monitor your opponent's reaction. If you landed a clean elbow, the majority of the time it will daze him further and knock him backward, creating an opening to conclude your combination with another powerful cross. Due to the powerful nature of each strike in the combo, the best time to use it is when your opponent is backed up against the cage because it prevents him from retreating from your strikes. When timed correctly, each strike will bounce your opponent off the cage and back into you, increasing the damage you cause.

Junie and I are in orthodox stances, searching for an opening to attack.

I step my left foot forward, rotate my hips in a counterclockwise direction, come up onto the ball of my right foot, and throw a right cross to Junie's jaw.

I pull my right arm back and reestablish my fighting stance.

Again I rotate my hips in a counterclockwise direction and come up onto the ball of my right foot, but this time I throw a rear side elbow to the side of Junie's face.

As Junie gets knocked back from my strike, I pull my arm back and reestablish my fighting stance.

For the third time, I rotate my hips and come up onto the ball of my right foot. Instead of throwing another rear side elbow, I return to the right cross.

Shawn Tompkins

Overhand - Head Control - Knee to Face

In this sequence, you throw a powerful overhand to close the distance between you and your opponent and turn his head to the side. Instead of pulling your arm back into your stance, you immediately wrap both of your hands around the back of his neck and pull his head downward. This will generate one of two reactions. If you're up against a striker, his first instinct will be to posture up and straighten his body to break your control. In such a situation, simply release your head control. As his chin pops up, immediately follow up with more strikes. However, when you obtain head control on a wrestler, his reaction will usually be the exact opposite. Instead of trying to posture up, he will most likely go with your downward pull by dropping his elevation and shooting in for a double-leg takedown as demonstrated in the sequence below. To capitalize on his reaction, switch your stance to put your lead leg behind you and then throw a powerful knee. With his face moving downward and your knee moving upward, it is a very powerful strike. A lot of times you'll knock your opponent out, but if you don't, you must again be prepared for two possible reactions. If he continues to shoot in for the takedown, pivot on your rear foot and circle your lead leg to the outside of his body. This will prevent him from snaring both of your legs and completing the double-leg, as well as give you a dominant angle of attack. If he realizes the danger he is in and attempts to pull away, release control of his head so that his chin pops up and then follow up with more strikes.

Junie and I are in orthodox stances, searching for an opening to attack.

Rotating my hips in a counterclockwise direction, I come up onto the ball of my right foot and throw an overhand right toward Junie's face.

Rotating my body slightly more than I would on a cross, I send my right fist on an arching trajectory into the side of Junie's face.

Instead of pulling my right arm back into my stance, I wrap my hand around the back of Junie's neck, securing a collar tie.

Driving Junie toward his right side using my right hand, I rotate my body in a clockwise direction and shoot my left hand toward the back of his head.

I place my left hand on the back of Junie's head, and then use both hands to force his head toward his right side to disrupt his balance.

Forcing Junie's head down using my hands, I leap into the air and switch the positioning of my feet. I accomplish this by moving my right leg forward and my left leg back.

I land in the exact same position, only now my left foot is positioned behind me.

Keeping Junie's head down using my hands, I drive my left knee upward toward his face.

I crash my left knee into Junie's face.

Shawn Tompkins

Jab - Side Elbow - Hook - Head Control - Knee

In this combination you employ both long-range and short-range strikes to keep your opponent guessing. Just as with many of the combos shown, this one begins with a jab to the face. The goal is to anger your opponent and get him to retaliate by moving into you, either with a punch of his own or to tie you up in the clinch. If he takes the bait, retain your fighting stance and immediately throw a side elbow with your rear arm. If he ignores the bait and moves away from you instead, then you will need to step your lead foot forward to close enough distance to land with the rear side elbow strike. Either way, it is important to throw a proper side elbow. You want to use the same dynamics as you would on a right-hand punch. To generate power, pivot on your rear foot, let that energy rise up, and then pivot your hips and shoulders together to throw the elbow. If you lean forward, you will not only jeopardize power in your strike, but you will also be out of position to throw your follow-up strike. By keeping your hips underneath your torso with the elbow, you will be able to immediately transition into a lead hook. If you look at the photos below, you'll notice that I keep my palm facing toward me when I throw the hook. As I mentioned in the basic technique section, utilizing this form allows you to dramatically turn your opponent's head, which is advantageous for two reasons. First, turning your opponent's head will often slosh his brain into his skull, shutting off his lights. If he absorbs the blow, his head will still be turned, allowing you to wrap your hand around the back of his neck and pull his head down into a knee strike.

Junie and I are in orthodox stances, searching for an opening to attack.

I throw a jab to Junie's face to shift his weight backward.

As I pull my left arm back into my stance, I rotate my hips in a counterclockwise direction, come up onto the ball of my right foot, and throw a rear side elbow toward Junie's head.

Continuing to rotate my hips in a counterclockwise direction, I throw a rear side elbow to Junie's jaw. Notice how my strike forces him to lean toward his right side.

I plant my right foot on the mat, come up onto the ball of my left foot, rotate my hips in a clockwise direction, and throw a lead hook toward Junie's jaw.

Pivoting on the ball of my left foot, I land a lead hook to the side of Junie's jaw.

Rotating my hips in a counterclockwise direction, I shoot my right hand to the right side of Junie's head and cup the back of his skull.

I reach my left arm forward and wrap it around the back of Junie's neck.

Forcing Junie's head down using my hands, I drive my right knee upward into his face.

Shawn Tompkins

Cross - Hook - Uppercut - Hook - Collar Tie Knee

This combination is similar to the previous one in that I utilize both long-range and close-range strikes, but instead of leading with a jab, I lead with a powerful cross. It is important to note that you can replace the cross with an overhand. Trying to decide which one to lead with should largely be based upon your opponent's skill level. While the overhand is a devastating strike, it is also very risky because you cross your rear arm to the opposite side of your body. If your opponent is a slick boxer with good head movement, I recommend sticking with the cross to avoid possible counters.

If you look at the photos below, you'll notice that when I throw the cross I step to the outside of my opponent's body. In addition to removing my head from my opponent's line of fire, it also gives me a dominant angle of attack, which allows me to immediately follow up with a lead hook. Striking the side of my opponent's jaw with the hook, his head turns toward the opposite side, creating an opening for me to throw a rear uppercut. Landing the uppercut to his chin, his head rises up, giving me an opportunity to strike the side of his jaw with a second lead hook. Just as with the initial hook, my opponent's head turns to the side. Instead of using that opening to land another punch, I wrap my hands around the back of his neck, pull his head down, and land a knee to his body.

Junie and I are in orthodox stances, searching for an opening to attack.

Rotating my hips in a counterclockwise direction, I come up onto the ball of my right foot and throw a cross to Junie's chin.

I plant my right foot on the mat, come up onto the ball of my left foot, and rotate my body in a clockwise direction.

Pivoting on the ball of my left foot, I land a lead hook to the right side of Junie's jaw.

After landing the hook, I continue to rotate my hips in a clockwise direction to prime my hips for a rear uppercut.

Rotating my hips in a counterclockwise direction, I come up onto the ball of my right foot and throw an uppercut toward Junie's jaw.

Continuing with my rotation, I throw my right fist upward between Junie's arms and strike his chin.

As I pull my right arm back into my stance, I plant my right foot on the mat, come up onto the ball of my left foot, and rotate my hips in a clockwise direction.

I land a lead hook to the right side of Junie's jaw.

I grab Junie's right wrist with my left hand to prevent him from throwing a cross. At the same time, I rotate my hips in a counter-clockwise direction, come up onto the ball of my right foot, and shoot my right hand forward and grab the back of his head.

I force Junie's head downward using my right hand and drive my right knee upward toward his midsection.

Pulling Junie's head down, I drive my right knee into his midsection.

Forrest Griffin

Missed Hook - Spinning Backfist - Pivot

As you have probably noticed by the techniques I put into this book, I like to throw a lot of lead hooks. It's a great strike because it often allows you to pivot to the outside of your opponent's body and establish a dominant angle of attack. The downside is that when you miss the strike due to your opponent leaning or stepping back, the momentum of the punch momentarily turns your back to him, making you vulnerable to takedowns and counterstrikes. In an attempt to make the best of a bad situation, I began throwing spinning backfists every time I missed my lead hook, and it worked surprisingly well. With my back turned, my opponent's natural reaction was to step forward and catch me in an awkward position, causing him to walk directly into the spinning backfist. When studying the photos, it is important to notice that I do not conclude the sequence upon landing the backfist. Unless you knock your opponent out, your back will still be turned to him. To prevent him from taking your back and doing all sorts of nasty things, you immediately want to pivot to the outside of his body as demonstrated below. This will remove you from his line of fire and give a dominant angle of attack, allowing you to follow up with more strikes.

Lance and I are in orthodox fighting stances, searching for an opening to attack.

I throw a lead hook toward the right side of Lance's face.

Lance evades my lead hook by leaning backward.

ELABORATE COMBINATIONS

I have missed the hook. To make the best out of a bad situation, I step my left foot toward the outside of Lance's lead leg and continue to rotate in a clockwise direction.

Pivoting on my left foot, I slide my right foot in a clockwise direction. At the same time, I throw a spinning back fist to the right side of Lance's head.

After landing the spinning back fist, I pivot on my right foot and slide my left foot across the mat in a clockwise direction to evade Lance's counters and acquire a dominant angle of attack.

Hook - Spinning Back Elbow

In the previous sequence I demonstrated how to follow up with a spinning backfist when you miss with a lead hook. The combo shown here comes into play when you land the lead hook and rattle your opponent, yet he doesn't back up. While he is dazed, you step your lead foot across your body and to the outside of his lead leg. This turns your back to your opponent and puts you in close range. If he still has his bearings after getting hit with the lead hook, it is possible for him to take your back and execute a takedown, so it is very important that you make sure that he is wounded before executing the technique. Once you have the proper foot positioning, rotate your body just as you did with the previous technique, but with minimal space between your bodies, follow up with a spinning back elbow instead of a spinning backfist. Again, it is very important to pivot to the outside of your opponent's body after completing the elbow strike to remove yourself from his line of fire and establish a dominant angle of attack.

Lance and I are in orthodox stances, searching for an opening to attack.

I throw a left hook to the side of Lance's head, but he elevates his right arm and blocks the strike.

Instead of pulling my left arm back into my stance, I move it toward the left side of Lance's body and continue to rotate in a clockwise direction.

I step my left foot to the outside of Lance's lead leg.

Continuing to rotate in a clockwise direction, I throw a spinning back elbow at the right side of Lance's head.

Immediately after landing the elbow, I pivot on my right foot and slide my left foot across the mat to evade Lance's attacks and acquire a dominant angle of attack.

Greg Jackson

Jab to Spinning Back Kick

In this sequence I demonstrate how to set up a spinning back kick using a jab. The goal is not to land the jab with all your strength, but rather to use it to pull your opponent's focus high and momentarily blind him with your fist. While his vision is obscured, you step your lead leg across your body and to the outside of your opponent's lead leg. Although this momentarily turns your back to your opponent, it also primes your hips to throw a spinning back kick to his midsection. The key to success with this combination is launching the back kick immediately after the jab. If you delay, your opponent will spot the kick coming and most likely move out of the way, leaving you in a compromising position. However, when you blend the two seamlessly together and land the kick, your opponent will most likely be in a good deal of pain.

My opponent and I are standing in orthodox stances, searching for an opening to attack.

To set up the spinning back kick, I throw a jab into my opponent's face. The goal is not to necessarily land the jab, but rather momentarily blind him. With his vision blocked, I step my left foot across my body and to the outside of his lead leg.

I pull my left arm back into my stance and rotate my body in a clockwise direction.

Shifting my weight onto my left leg, I lean back and throw a back kick into my opponent's solar plexus.

Parry Jab - Cross - Lead Hook

In this sequence you and your opponent are in the same fighting stance and he throws a jab. Instead of slipping his punch, you parry it to the outside of your body using your rear hand, making it difficult for him to follow up with a cross. While his arm is still outstretched, you slide your rear hand down his arm, shoot it over his shoulder, and land a hook to the side of his face. If you look at the photos below, you'll notice that when I execute the punch I rotate my body and lean into it. While leaning can often get you in trouble when launching an attack, it is much safer in this scenario. Having parried your opponent's arm to the outside of your body, he is in an awkward position, making it difficult for him to launch a counterattack with his right hand. Leaning into the punch and rotating your body also primes your hips to follow up with a lead hook to your opponent's liver. The key to success with this technique is flowing into the initial hook directly off the parry. Instead of viewing the parry and hook as two separate techniques, they should be treated as one fluid movement. If you hesitate between them, your opponent will pull his arm back into his stance, not only making it difficult to land your first strike, but also making you vulnerable to your opponent's right hand.

Junie and I are in orthodox stances, searching for an opening to attack.

As Junie throws a jab, I rotate my body in a counterclockwise direction and move my right hand toward his arm.

Coming up onto the ball of my right foot, I parry Junie's arm toward the outside of my body.

Instead of pulling my right arm back into my stance, I throw an overhand right over Junie's outstretched arm and into the side of his face.

I drop my elevation and rotate my body in a clockwise direction.

Continuing to rotate in a clockwise direction, I throw a left hook to Junie's sternum.

Shawn Tompkins

Parry Jab - Switch Step - Mid Round Kick

This combination is employed in the same scenario as the last—you and your opponent are in the same fighting stance and he throws a jab at your face. Just as in the previous combo, you parry his jab to the outside of your body, but instead of throwing a hook over the top of his outstretched arm, you keep your rear palm glued to his wrist and execute a switch step. The danger with this technique is getting hit with a cross while executing the switch step, but before your opponent can throw the cross, he must first pull his jab back into his stance. By maintaining contact with his outstretched arm, you can gauge exactly when the cross might be coming. The reason for executing the switch step is to create more distance between your lead leg and his rib cage, which in turn allows you to deliver a more powerful kick. Remember, distance and speed equals power. As he throws the cross, you lean back to avoid getting hit with his punch and launch a round kick at his exposed ribs and liver.

Junie and I are in orthodox stances, searching for an opening to attack.

As Junie throws a jab, I come up onto the ball of my right foot, rotate my body in a counterclockwise direction, and parry his arm toward the outside of my body using my right hand.

Immediately after parrying Junie's jab, I execute a switch step by hopping upward, moving my lead foot back, and my rear foot forward.

I land in a southpaw stance.

Pivoting on the ball of my right foot, I rotate my hips in a clockwise direction and throw a left round kick toward Junie's midsection.

I deliver a left round kick to Junie's midsection.

Shawn Yarborough

Parry Jab to Rear Side Elbow

In this sequence I demonstrate how to parry your opponent's jab downward using your lead hand and then follow up with a rear side elbow strike to the side of his face. The key to success with this technique is throwing the elbow strike before your opponent can pull his arm back into his stance and protect his head. While it is possible to accomplish this using a regular parry, I like to drive his arm downward to increase the time it takes for him to retract his arm. I also like to maintain contact with his jab arm until I have already begun throwing the elbow strike.

Erich and I are in orthodox stances, searching for an opening to attack.

Erich throws a jab.

I parry Erich's jab downward using my left hand. At the same time, I begin rotating my hips in a counterclockwise direction and elevate my right elbow.

Continuing to rotate in a counterclockwise direction, I arch my right elbow downward toward Erich's face.

I land a rear side elbow to Erich's jaw.

Shawn Yarborough

Parry Jab - Parry Cross - Head Control - Knee

In this sequence I demonstrate how to parry the common jab/cross combination and then transition into a knee strike. Instead of parrying my opponent's jab downward as I did in the previous combination, I parry it toward the inside of his body using my rear hand. I don't use any extreme hand movements—all I do is simply tap the outside of his extending arm to redirect his punch away from my face. As he pulls his arm back into his body, he immediately launches a cross. Again I parry his punch toward the inside of his body, this time using my lead hand. However, instead of just tapping his arm to redirect it, I maintain contact with his arm using my palm to hinder him from pulling his arm back toward his body. At the same time, I throw my rear hand forward just as I would when throwing a cross, but rather than punching him in the face, I shoot my hand past his head and hook it around the back of his neck. Forcing my opponent off balance using both of my hands, I throw a rear knee strike to his abdomen.

Erich and I are in orthodox stances, searching for an opening to attack.

As Erich throws a jab, I parry his fist toward the inside of his body using my rear hand.

Erich follows up with a cross, and I parry his arm toward the inside of his body using my left hand.

Instead of releasing my parry, I continue to apply pressure using my left hand and force Erich's arm across his body. At the same time, I shoot my right arm forward and hook my hand around the back of his neck.

I drive my right knee toward Erich's midsection.

I land a right knee strike to Erich's midsection.

Forrest Griffin

Countering the Cross with Lead Hook

In this sequence I demonstrate an excellent method for evading and countering the ever-popular jab/cross combination. To begin, I use my rear hand to parry my opponent's jab to the outside of my body. Next, my opponent launches a right cross. To evade his shot, I step my lead foot to the outside of his rear leg, pivot on the ball of my lead foot, and rotate my hips and shoulders in a clockwise direction. This turns the side of my body toward him and removes my head from his line of fire. At the same time, I use my pivot and rotation to launch a long lead hook to the side of his face. The key to success with this technique is landing the hook while your opponent's cross arm is still outstretched. If you lag with your punch, he will most likely pull his arm back into his body and block your lead hook.

Lance and I are in orthodox stances, searching for an opening to attack.

Lance steps his lead foot forward and throws a jab. To evade his strike, I lean slightly back and catch his fist in my right palm.

As Lance follows up with a cross, I pivot on the ball of my left foot, rotate my hips in a clockwise direction, and throw a lead hook over his outstretched arm and into the side of his face.

COUNTERING THE CROSS

THE ULTIMATE MIXED MARTIAL ARTIST

Evade Cross with Lean Back - Cross Counter

This is another excellent technique for evading the common jab/cross combination. Just as in previous sequences, I block my opponent's jab using a rear parry. However, instead of pivoting my hips to evade his cross, I push off my lead leg and shoot my body backward. It's possible to remain planted and evade the cross with a simple lean back, but it requires nail-sharp timing and an excellent sense of distance. If you are off by even an inch, you will eat a powerful cross to the face. Personally, I prefer leaping backward to ensure I avoid the cross. As my opponent pulls his cross-arm back into his body, I drive off my rear leg, lean forward, and deliver a cross of my own to the side of his face. The key to success with this technique is throwing your cross while your opponent is in the process of retracting his arm. If you delay, he will block your strike using his arms.

Lance and I are in orthodox stances, searching for an opening to attack.

Lance steps forward and throws a jab. I block his strike by leaning slightly back and catching his fist in my right hand.

Lance follows his jab with a cross. To evade his strike, I push off my lead foot and shoot my body backward.

As my right foot touches down, I shift my weight onto my rear leg to avoid Lance's cross.

As Lance pulls his right arm back into his stance, I push off my right foot, rotate my body in a counterclockwise direction, and throw a right cross.

Before Lance can pull his arm back into his stance, I land a right cross to his face.

Slip Cross - Lead Hook to Body - Cross

In this scenario I'm standing in the same fighting stance as my opponent and he unleashes a right cross at my face. As demonstrated in the basic techniques at the beginning of the book, I rotate my hips and slip to the outside of the punch, causing him to miss his strike. With my opponent's weight positioned in front of his lead knee, he is in a terrible position to follow up with another strike, and with his rear arm outstretched, his ribs and liver are vulnerable. To capitalize on his awkward positioning, I uncoil my hips and deliver a powerful shovel hook to his liver. To cause as much damage as possible, I corkscrew my fist just prior to impact and strike at an upward angle of forty-five degrees, sending a shock wave through his body and out his far shoulder. Instinctively, my opponent leans toward his right and lowers his arms to protect his liver from taking further damage, creating a unobstructed pathway for my follow-up cross.

Junie and I are in orthodox stances, searching for an opening to attack.

Junie throws a right cross. To evade his strike, I shift my weight onto my left leg, rotate my hips in a counterclockwise direction, and begin moving my head toward my left side.

Continuing with my former actions, Junie's cross slips by the right side of my head.

With my hips spring-loaded from having slipped Junie's cross, I unwind them by rotating in a clockwise direction and throw a lead shovel hook to his liver.

Rotating my hips in a counterclockwise direction, I throw a cross toward Junie's chin.

I land a cross to Junie's chin.

Shawn Tompkins

Jab - Cross - Evade Hook - Rear Hook - Lead Hook

As I mentioned earlier, when you throw the traditional jab/cross combination, a lot of opponents will immediately retaliate with a looping punch. In this scenario, I use this common reaction to my advantage. From an opposite fighting stance, I throw a jab/cross to bait my opponent into throwing a rear left hook. To evade his shot, I step my rear foot to the outside of his body, drop my level, and weave underneath his punch. When I pop back up into my fighting stance, my situation has improved greatly. My outward step has provided me with a dominant angle of attack, and due to my opponent's circular rotation, the left side of his face is exposed. To capitalize, I throw a rear hook to either the side of his jaw or the soft spot behind his ear. This pushes his head to his left side, directly into my follow-up lead hook. When utilized properly, this is a very high percentage KO combination. Ray Sefo uses this technique a lot in K-1. He's a little shorter than the majority of K-1 heavyweights, so he uses the jab/cross to get his opponents to counter with the hook. Evading the hook causes his opponent to spin around, and he catches him behind the ear with a hook, often resulting in a knockout.

1 Junie is in a southpaw stance, and I'm in an orthodox stance. Both of us are searching for an opening to attack.

2 I throw a jab to Junie's face.

3 Rotating my hips in a counterclockwise direction, I come up onto the ball of my right foot and throw a cross toward Junie's jaw.

4 I land my cross.

5 I pull my right arm back into my stance and prepare to launch my next strike.

6 Before I can launch another attack, Junie throws a rear hook toward my head. To evade his strike, I step my rear foot forward and drop my elevation.

As I drop my elevation and shift my weight to my right leg, Junie's hook sails over the top of my head.

I increase my elevation, putting me to the outside of Junie's body.

I rotate my hips in a counterclockwise direction, come up onto the ball of my right foot, and throw a rear hook toward the left side of Junie's head.

I connect with my hook, forcing Junie's head toward his right side.

Planting my right foot on the mat, I rotate my hips in a clockwise direction and throw a left hook toward the right side of Junie's jaw.

Continuing to rotate in a clockwise direction, I come up onto the ball of my left foot and land a hook to Junie's jaw.

Shawn Tompkins

Evade Hook - Cross - Lead Hook - Cross

In this scenario, my opponent and I are in the same fighting stance and he throws a lead hook. Instead of weaving underneath the punch as I would if he threw a rear hook, I evade his shot by simply dropping my level. At the same time, I throw a right cross to his solar plexus, which is exposed due to his circular punch. It is important to notice in the photos below that I do not lean into the cross, but rather keep my hips underneath my shoulders. As my opponent leans forward due to the solar plexus shot, my sturdy base allows me to pop back up and deliver a lead hook to the side of his jaw or behind his ear. Getting knocked off balance, my opponent's first instinct is to elevate his arms to protect his head from taking further damage. Switching things up, I again drop my level and deliver a powerful cross to his solar plexus.

Junie and I are in orthodox stances, searching for an opening to attack.

As Junie throws a lead hook, I drop my elevation by bending my knees.

As Junie's hook approaches, I rotate my hips in a counterclockwise direction, come up onto the ball of my right foot, and throw a cross to his body.

I increase my elevation and throw a lead hook to the right side of Junie's jaw.

To keep Junie guessing, I drop my level again by bending my knees.

Rotating my hips in a counterclockwise direction and coming up onto the ball of my right foot, I throw another cross to Junie's body.

Shawn Tompkins

Block Hook - Lead Side Elbow - Rear Side Elbow

When you're pinned up against the cage and your opponent unleashes with strikes, it can be difficult to employ evasive tactics due to your lack of mobility. To avoid taking shots directly to the face, you're forced to block the punches using your arms. However, you can't just sit there and block all day long because eventually one of your opponent's fists will find a crack in your guard and connect solidly with your head or face. To prevent such an outcome, I like to utilize aggressive blocking tactics such as the one demonstrated in the sequence below. My opponent sees that I'm off balance or in an awkward position and throws a lead hook at the side of my head. To block the hook, I elevate my right arm to the side of my head and rotate my hips away from the punch. This last step is very important because in addition to softening the blow, it also primes my hips to throw a powerful elbow strike from my opposite side. Combinations such as this one are important to train because they can get you out of a tight spot. Instead of blocking the strike and reverting into defensive mode, you use your block to set up an attack.

Junie and I are fighting in close range. Both of us are in orthodox stances

As Junie throws a lead hook toward the right side of my head, I elevate my right arm to block his punch.

I place my right hand behind my right ear and rotate my body in a counterclockwise direction to lessen the blow.

With my hips spring-loaded from my outside block, I rotate them in a clockwise direction and throw a lead side elbow toward the side of Junie's jaw.

The tip of my left elbow connects with the side of Junie's jaw, turning his head toward his left side.

I rotate my hips in a counterclockwise direction and elevate my right elbow.

Coming up onto the ball of my right foot, I continue to rotate my hips in a counterclockwise direction and throw a right side elbow into the side of Junie's jaw.

Check Round Kick - Counter with Round Kick

This is a very basic and common Muay Thai combination that transitions well to mixed martial arts. It begins by checking your opponent's rear Thai kick using your lead leg. However, instead of dropping your foot straight down to the canvas and reestablishing your stance after checking the kick, you shoot your lead leg behind you. The instant your foot touches down, you push off the mat, rotate your hips, and deliver a lead round kick to your opponent's midsection. The goal is to land your kick while your opponent is still retracting his, making it very difficult for him to check your strike.

Erich and I are in orthodox stances, searching for an opening to attack.

As Erich elevates his right leg to throw a rear around kick, I shift my weight onto my right leg and lift my lead foot off the mat.

To block Erich's round kick, I lift my left leg, angle my knee toward the outside of my body, and catch his leg on my shin.

Instead of dropping my left foot straight down to the mat, I shoot it behind me to establish a southpaw stance. Notice how I performed this action while Erich is still pulling his leg back into his stance.

As Erich's right foot touches down, I rotate my hips in a clockwise direction, pivot on the ball of my right foot, and throw a left round kick to his liver. Notice how I have extended my left arm across Erich's body to prevent him from throwing punches.

Shawn Yarborough

Check Round Kick - Cross - Hook - Low Kick

When you check your opponent's round kick, it takes him longer to pull his kicking leg back into his stance than it does for you to drop the foot of your checking leg down to the canvas. This means that you reestablish your base and balance quicker than your opponent, making it a good time to launch an attack. In this sequence, I demonstrate how to capitalize on your opponent's slow recovery by throwing a cross, a lead hook, and then a low round kick to the outside of his lead leg.

Erich and I are in orthodox stances, searching for an opening to attack.

As Erich elevates his right leg to throw a round kick, I shift my weight to my right leg.

I elevate my left leg, angle my knee toward the outside of my body at a forty-five degree angle, and catch Erich's kick on my shin.

I drop my left foot to the mat, rotate my hips in a counterclockwise direction, and throw a cross.

I plant my right foot on the mat, come up onto the ball of my left foot, rotate my hips in a clockwise direction, and throw a lead hook.

I land a left hook to Erich's jaw.

I rotate my hips in a counterclockwise direction, come up onto the ball of my right foot, and reach my right hand forward as though I'm throwing a cross.

I place my right hand on Erich's chest to prevent him from throwing punches and shift my weight onto my left leg.

Rotating my hips in a counterclockwise direction, I pivot on the ball of my left foot and land a round kick to the outside of Erich's left leg.

Block Round Kick - Cross - Hook - Knee

This is another example of how to employ an aggressive block. In this scenario, my opponent throws a round kick to my midsection, and I rotate my body toward the kick and block it using my arms. With my hips already spring-loaded, I do not return to my fighting stance. Instead, I immediately uncoil my hips and throw a right cross. This allows me to strike my opponent while he is still on one leg. As he gets knocked backward, his hands drop, allowing me to follow up with a lead hook to the side of his jaw. The lead hook pushes my opponent toward the power side of my body, creating a perfect opportunity to conclude with a powerful rear knee to his midsection. The key to success with this combination is immediately transitioning to the cross off your block. When you hit your opponent while he is on one leg, he'll have a very difficult time catching up to your combination. As a result, his only defense will be to drop to the canvas. If you're going to be fighting a Thai boxer who likes to set up his combinations with kicks, I strongly suggest practicing this technique.

Junie and I are in orthodox stances, searching for an opening to attack.

Junie switches his stance by moving his rear leg forward and his lead leg back.

Junie lands in a southpaw stance.

As Junie rotates his hips in a clockwise direction and throws a left round kick toward my midsection, I rotate my body in a clockwise direction to block his kick using my arms.

5

I catch Junie's kick using both of my forearms.

6

As Junie pulls his leg back, I rotate my body in a counterclockwise direction.

7

Continuing to rotate in a counterclockwise direction, I come up onto the ball of my rear foot and throw a right hook to Junie's jaw.

8

As I pull my right arm back, I rotate my body in a clockwise direction and prepare to throw a lead hook.

9

Planting my right foot on the mat, I pivot on the ball of my left foot and land a left hook to Junie's jaw.

10

Shifting my weight onto my left leg, I drive my right knee into Junie's midsection.

Shawn Tompkins

Evade Lead-Leg Kick with Switch Step - Round Kick

This is an excellent technique to use when up against a fighter who likes to throw kicks to the inside of your lead leg. For the best results, it should be employed after your opponent has already landed a couple of these kicks because his confidence will be up and he'll most likely put some decent power into it. The instant he launches his kick, reverse your stance by stepping your lead foot behind you. When timed right, your opponent will miss his kick entirely. And if he committed to the kick, the momentum of his leg will rotate his body and disrupt his balance. With his lead leg now in the rear, you're in a perfect position to capitalize on his awkard stance by launching a round kick into his midsection.

Junie and I are in orthodox stances, searching for an opening to attack.

Junie steps his rear foot forward and to the outside of my lead leg, telling me he is about to throw a round kick to the inside of my lead leg.

Instead of checking Junie's kick, I step my left foot behind me, causing him to miss his strike.

Junie is thrown off balance from missing his kick.

Before Junie can reestablish his stance, I rotate my hips in a clockwise direction, pivot on the ball of my right foot, and throw a left round kick toward his midsection.

I land my left round kick to Junie's midsection.

Shawn Tompkins

Check Kick - Switch Step - Head Control - Knee - Elbow

In this sequence, my opponent throws a rear round low kick and I check it using my lead leg. In order for him to launch another strike, he must first pull his leg back toward his body and reestablish his fighting stance, and this will take him a moment to accomplish. In the interim, I execute a switch step to reverse my stance and hook my hands around the back of his neck. Once accomplished, I pull his head down and land a powerful knee strike to his sternum. Instinctively leaning forward and dropping his arms to protect his body, I conclude with a rear elbow to the side of his head. The key to success with this technique is switching your stance immediately after checking the kick. There are two ways to do this. In the sequence below, I drop my foot back to the mat and then execute the switch step, which is the easier of the two. If speed is of the essence, instead of dropping your foot to the mat after checking the kick, immediately throw it behind you, as Shawn Yarborough demonstrated in an earlier combo.

Junie and I are in orthodox stances, searching for an opening to attack.

As Junie throws a rear round kick toward the outside of my lead leg, I lift my left foot off the mat, angle my knee toward the outside of my body, and catch his kick with my shin.

I drop my left foot to the mat.

I execute a switch step my hopping upward, moving my rear foot forward, and my lead foot back.

COUNTERING KICKS

I land in a southpaw stance.

I lean forward, come up onto the ball of my left foot, and shoot my hands toward the back of Junie's head.

I hook my right hand around the back of Junie's neck and my left hand around the back of his head.

As I force Junie's head downward using my hands, I drive my left knee into his midsection.

Still pushing down on Junie's head using my left hand, I pull my right arm back to deliver a side elbow.

I drop my left foot to the mat, rotate my hips in a counterclockwise direction, and deliver a side elbow to Junie's head.

THE ULTIMATE MIXED MARTIAL ARTIST

Shawn Yarborough

Catch Round Kick - Cross

In this sequence my opponent throws a rear round kick aimed at my midsection. Instead of checking his kick, I turn my body away from the incoming strike to lessen the impact and then wrap my near arm around his calf muscle to catch his leg. Once accomplished, there is a broad array of attacks that you can implement. In this particular scenario, I choose to capitalize on my opponent's awkward positioning by throwing a cross. One thing you must keep in mind when catching your opponent's round kicks is that it can oftentimes be difficult to tell the difference between a mid-kick and a head kick. If you misread the target and drop your hand to catch his leg, there is a good chance that you'll take a kick to the side of the head.

Erich and I are in orthodox stances, searching for an opening to attack.

Erich elevates his right knee, telling me that he is about to throw a rear round kick to my midsection. To prepare my defense, I step my right foot toward my right side.

As Erich throws his kick, I move my body away from it to lessen the impact. Next, I drop my left arm and wrap it around his calf muscle, catching his leg.

Maintaining a tight grip on Erich's right leg, I rotate my hips in a counterclockwise direction and throw a cross at his face.

Shawn Yarborough

Catch Round Kick - Rear Knee

This combination is very similar to the previous one in that I catch my opponent's rear round kick and then immediately shoot my rear arm forward, but instead of hitting him with a cross, I extend my hand past his head and secure a collar tie. This allows me to pull his head into me as I throw a rear knee to his midsection. Personally, I like to use this particular combo when I'm up against an opponent with an iron chin because it devastates the body.

Erich and I are in orthodox stances, searching for an opening to attack.

Erich elevates his right knee, telling me that he is about to throw a rear round kick to my midsection. To prepare my defense, I step my right foot toward my right side.

As Erich throws his kick, I move my body away from it to lessen the impact. Next, I drop my left arm and wrap it around his calf muscle, catching his leg.

Maintaining a tight grip on Erich's right leg, I rotate my hips in a counterclockwise direction, reach my right arm forward, and hook my hand around the back of his neck.

Pulling Erich's head down using my right hand, I drive my right knee into his solar plexus.

Shawn Yarborough

Catch Round Kick - Leg Sweep

In this sequence I catch my opponent's mid round-house kick, but instead of striking his face or midsection, I step my rear foot forward to close the distance between us and kick his grounded leg out from underneath him using my lead leg. Although this technique doesn't cause your opponent as much damage as the previous two, it looks great to the judges and is an excellent option when you want to bring the fight to the ground.

Erich and I are in orthodox stances, searching for an opening to attack.

Erich elevates his right knee, telling me that he is about to throw a rear round kick to my midsection. To prepare my defense, I step my right foot toward my right side.

As Erich throws his kick, I move my body away from it to lessen the impact. Next, I drop my left arm and wrap it around his calf muscle, catching his leg.

Maintaining a tight grip on Erich's right leg, I step my right leg forward to close the distance between us.

Rotating my hips in a clockwise direction, I throw a left round kick to the back of Erich's grounded leg.

Following through with my kick, Erich is swept off his feet.

Anuwat Kaewsamrit

Catch Front Kick - Leg Sweep

In this sequence my opponent throws a front kick at my lead hip. Instead of checking his kick, I step back, shift my weight onto my rear leg, and then drop my lead hand and grab his Achilles' tendon. It can be very difficult to keep an opponent's leg trapped with this simple grip for a prolonged period of time, so I immediately counter by throwing a rear round kick to the calf of his grounded leg. At the same time, I shoot my free arm in front of his body and push on his chest. The combination of these actions sweeps my opponent's grounded leg out from underneath him, causing him to fall to the mat.

My opponent and I are in orthodox stances, searching for an opening to attack.

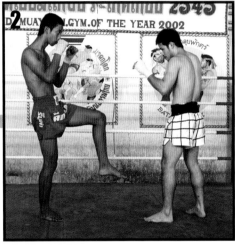

My opponent elevates his lead leg to throw a push kick.

To evade my opponent's kick, I shift my weight onto my rear leg and lean back. As his leg extends, I drop my left arm and cup my hand around his Achilles tendon, catching his leg.

Before my opponent can jerk his leg from my grasp, I move into him and begin rotating my body in a counterclockwise direction.

Pivoting on the ball of my left foot, I throw a right round kick into the back of my opponent's grounded leg. At the same time, I shoot my right arm in front of his body and push him backward. The combination of these actions sweeps his grounded leg out from underneath him and causes him to fall to his back.

Shawn Yarborough

Catch Front Kick - Lead Hook

This is another excellent option for countering your opponent's push kick. Just as Anuwat did in the previous sequence, I take a small step backward and redistribute my weight onto my rear leg the instant I see the kick coming. This takes me out of range and makes it easier for me to wrap my lead hand around the back of his ankle and catch his leg. Once accomplished, I disrupt his balance by pulling his trapped leg into me and then release control of his foot. As long as you pull hard enough, your opponent will fall forward. To capitalize on this awkward positioning, I like to step forward and throw a lead hook to the side of my opponent's face.

Erich and I are in orthodox stances, searching for an opening to attack.

Erich elevates his lead leg, alerting me to the fact that he is either going to throw a lead round kick or a lead push kick. To prepare myself for both, I shift my weight on to my rear leg and make my lead foot light on the mat.

Erich throws a lead push kick. To evade his strike, I lean slightly back, causing him to miss. As his leg extends, I drop my left arm and cup my hand around the back of his Achilles tendon, catching his leg. It is important to notice that my hand is cupped around the inside of his leg rather than the outside of his leg.

Keeping a tight grip on his leg, I pull Erich's leg into me using my left hand, disrupting his balance. At the same time, I step my left foot forward.

I release my grip on Erich's left leg. Having destroyed his base, he has no choice but to fall forward. As he drops, I rotate my body in a clockwise direction and throw a left hook toward the left side of his jaw.

Before Erich can reestablish his base and balance, I land a left hook to his jaw.

Shawn Yarborough

Evade Front Kick - Kick - Hook - Cross - Uppercut - Cross

This is another method for evading your opponent's push kick and then launching a counterattack. Just as with the previous technique, I move backward to cause my opponent to miss his kick and then trap his leg by cupping my hand around his Achilles tendon. However, instead of positioning my arm to the inside of his leg, I position it to the outside of his leg. This allows me to throw his leg toward the inside of his body, disrupting his balance. As he attempts to recover, I launch a rear round kick to the back of his lead leg. With my opponent in pain and his base thoroughly shattered, I deliver a lead hook, a cross, an uppercut, and then another cross.

1 Lance and I are in orthodox stances, searching for an opening to attack.

2 Lance elevates his lead leg, alerting me to the fact that he is either going to throw a lead round kick or a lead push kick. To prepare myself for both, I shift my weight on to my rear leg and make my lead foot light on the mat.

3 Lance throws a lead push kick. To evade his strike, I lean slightly back, causing him to miss. As his leg extends, I drop my left arm and cup my hand around the back of his Achilles tendon, catching his leg. However, it is important to notice that in this technique my arm is positioned to the outside of his leg.

4 I throw Lance's left leg toward the outside of my body, disrupting his balance.

5 As Lance attempts to reestablish his base, I step my left foot toward my left side and begin rotating my hips in a counterclockwise direction.

6 Pivoting on the ball of my left foot, I throw a right round kick to the backside of Lance's left leg.

I let the impact of my kick push my leg back into my fighting stance, and then rotate my hips and shoulders in a counterclockwise direction to spring-load my hips.

I rotate my hips in a clockwise direction, pivot on the ball of my left foot, and throw a lead hook toward the right side of Lance's jaw.

I land a lead hook to Lance's jaw.

I plant my left foot on the mat, rotate my hips in a counterclockwise direction, come up onto the ball of my right foot, and throw a right cross toward the left side of Lance's jaw.

I land my cross on Lance's jaw.

Rotating my hips in a clockwise direction, I throw a left uppercut toward Lance's chin.

I strike Lance's chin with my uppercut, lifting his head.

With Lance's chin exposed, I rotate my hips in a counterclockwise direction and throw a cross toward his face.

I land my cross to the left side of Lance's jaw.

Shawn Tompkins

Block Knee with Elbow - Hook - Collar Tie - Knee

This technique comes in handy when up against a good Thai boxer who likes to throw knees. It also works great when up against an opponent who is worried about your wrestling skills and constantly throws knees in an attempt to knock you out as you shoot in for a takedown. The goal is to punish your opponent every time he throws a knee. To accomplish this, you rotate into the knee strike and drive your elbow down into the top of his leg. When you land the elbow with power, it will separate the two muscles on the top of your opponent's leg, deaden the nerves, and cause him to momentarily freeze up. To capitalize on his stunned state, you increase your elevation, uncoil your hips, and deliver a lead hook to the side of his jaw. This pushes his body to the side, allowing you to shoot your rear hand forward, wrap it around the back of his neck, and then pull his head down into a rear knee. However, it is important to note that this is just one combination that you can do off the initial block. If you're a good wrestler and your goal is to take the fight to the ground, shooting in off the knee block is an excellent choice. When you're up against a fighter like Yves Edwards, you can pretty much expect him to knee every time you shoot in. Instead of risking getting knocked out, you drop your level, block his knee, and then shoot in.

Junie and I are in orthodox stances, searching for an opening to attack.

Junie leans forward to throw a rear knee. Immediately I begin dropping my level by bending my knees.

As Junie's knee approaches, I rotate in a counterclockwise direction, come up onto the ball of my right foot, and strike the top of his leg using a downward elbow.

Having wounded Junie's leg, I increase my elevation, rotate my body in a clockwise direction, and throw a left hook.

Pivoting on the ball of my left foot, I hit Junie with a lead hook.

As I pull my left arm back, I rotate my hips in a counterclockwise direction and come up onto the ball of my right foot.

I shoot my right arm forward and wrap it around the back of Junie's head.

I shoot my left hand forward and place it on the top of Junie's head.

Pulling Junie's head down using both hands, I drive my right knee into his face.

Part Two
Striking to the Takedown and Takedown Defense

STRIKING TO THE DOUBLE-LEG TAKEDOWN
(p. 149-157)

In today's MMA game it is strikingly obvious that you cannot simply shoot blindly in for a takedown. If you try, your opponent will see your shot coming and defend against it with strikes or another form of takedown defense. You must set up your takedowns with strikes or execute them after countering your opponent's strikes, plain and simple. However, striking for the takedown is different from striking to knock your opponent out. If you are looking for the knockout, your sense of distance and timing are crucial because you want to keep your opponent on the end of your punches. If your goal is to score a takedown, sense of distance and timing aren't as important. Your main goal with your punches is to pull your opponent's focus high. While he is distracted, you drop your elevation, close the distance between you and your opponent, and obtain control of his legs. This is not to say that you don't need to be accurate with your punches. Although you might not be looking to knock him out, you must still threaten your opponent with your strikes. However, with the takedown being your primary goal, you don't want to jeopardize your positioning with your strikes. While it is important to learn the difference between these two methods of striking, it is also important to develop them both. The goal in an fight is to be as unpredictable as possible. If you conclude every combination you throw with a takedown, your opponent will automatically be on the lookout for a takedown and prepare his defenses. And if you never shoot in for a takedown, your opponent will eliminate that worry from his mind, which allows him to focus more on defending against your strikes. No matter what your goal is in a fight, you must constantly switch things up to keep your opponent guessing.

When studying the techniques in this section, it is important to pay close attention to body positioning. The goal when shooting in for a double-leg takedown is to square your hips with your opponent's hips so you can penetrate in and seize control of both of his legs. As you will notice, some of the strikes in the upcoming combinations stagger your hips with your opponent's hips. They leave you in somewhat of an awkward position, making it important to reset your base before shooting in. Other strikes allow you to flow directly into the takedown without resetting your base. While the latter is certainly more favorable because it leads to a quicker transition, both types of combinations have their place. It is also important to note that the majority of the time, you will execute double-leg takedowns when you are in the same fighting stance, meaning you have the same foot forward. With both of your feet staggered, your opponent's body is one big target that you can drive into. When you are in opposite fighting stances, your opponent's lead leg is positioned directly in front of your lead arm, making the single-leg your primary takedown.

STRIKING TO THE SINGLE-LEG TAKEDOWN
(p. 159-160)

This section demonstrates two methods for setting up the single-leg takedown utilizing strikes. In the first combination you throw a lead hook to distract your opponent, obtain control of his lead leg, and then pull it up to your chest to secure the single-leg position. Although there are many ways to complete the single-leg from this position, the running-the-pipe method shown here is by far the most common and effective. The second combination not only demonstrates how to set up the single-leg takedown utilizing the cross, but also how to complete the takedown when your opponent prevents you from establishing the single-leg position by sprawling his legs back.

COUNTERING STRIKES TO THE TAKEDOWN
(p. 162-164)

In addition to learning how to set up your takedowns with strikes, it is also mandatory to learn how to setup takedowns by evading your opponent's strikes. In many cases, this is the most effective way to secure a takedown. When you cause your opponent to miss with a punch, he will often overextend. His guard will be broken and his balance will be compromised. To make the most of his vulnerability, you drop your level low and penetrate in for his legs before he can reestablish his stance. To help you down this road, this section offers two methods for countering strikes to the takedown. The first one is based on evading your opponent's jab, and the second one is based on evading his cross. The most important thing with both of these methods is shooting in for the takedown before your opponent can pull his extended arm back into his stance. The majority of the time your opponent won't just throw a single strike—he will throw a multi-punch combination. If you do not shoot in prior to him pulling his punching arm back into you stance, there is a good chance that you will walk straight into the second strike in his combination.

DEFENDING TAKEDOWNS WITH STRIKES
(p. 165-170)

This section demonstrates various ways to defend against your opponent's takedowns utilizing knees and uppercuts. With each of these techniques, timing is crucial. The goal is to land your strike as your opponent drops his level and shoots, causing the downward momentum of his body to meet the upward momentum of your strike. In order to pull this off, your defense has to be instinctual. If you stop to think about what you have to do, it will be too late. Your opponent will have closed the distance and put you on your back. And even when you time your shot perfectly, using strikes to defend against takedowns is still risky. A lot of opponents have very tough chins, and if you fail to knock them out, they will often follow through with the takedown. As you will see in the upcoming section, there are ways to mitigate your risk by cutting angles off to the side of his body and even landing follow-up strikes to prevent your opponent from reshooting, but even then you must still accept a certain amount of risk. Before the fight, it is important to weigh the risks versus the rewards.

If you are up against an opponent who has exceptional skills on the ground, it is probably in your best interest to utilize one of the safer takedown defenses shown later in the book, such as the sprawl.

DEFENDING AGAINST THE DOUBLE-LEG TAKEDOWN
(p. 171-184)

The double-leg is the most common takedown utilized in MMA, making it mandatory that you learn how to defend against it. Although this can oftentimes seem like a grueling task, takedowns deserve the same amount of attention as strikes or submissions. After all, you wouldn't spend all your time learning how to throw strikes without learning how to counter them. Takedowns should be viewed in the same light. To help you down this road, this section covers numerous takedowns from both the same and opposite stance as your opponent. While your opponent will most often shoot for double-legs when in the same stance, a lot of opponents will shoot for the double when in opposite stances, making it important to learn how to defend against both. With all these techniques, the quickness of your reactions is of the utmost importance. The goal is to halt your opponent's penetration before he can gain control of your hips. If you fail to do this, defending against his takedown becomes a whole lot more difficult to achieve.

DEFENDING AGAINST THE SINGLE-LEG TAKEDOWN
(p. 186-199)

This section covers a number of countering options for when your opponent snatches up your lead leg and obtains the single-leg position. You will learn how to escape the position by attacking your opponent's grips. You will learn how to use his positioning to execute a takedown of your own. You will learn how to attack his vulnerable neck and legs with submission holds, and you will even learn how to execute a flying attack. The key to success with all of these techniques is beginning your counter the instant your opponent snatches up your leg. If you allow your opponent to hike your leg up to his chest and disrupt your balance, your chances of employing a successful counter drop significantly.

Jon Fitch

Striking to Double-Leg Takedown

In this sequence I demonstrate how to set up a double-leg takedown utilizing a jab. As mentioned in the introduction to this section, shooting in blindly from the outside is almost always a recipe for disaster. Your opponent will most likely see your shot coming for a mile and counter by either striking or sprawling. With your entire body moving forward, if your opponent strikes, there is a good chance that you will go to sleep. And if he sprawls and you get stuck underneath his body, there are all sorts of nasty things he can do, such as circling around your body to take your back. Setting up your strikes using takedowns is a much, much better option. The goal is to distract your opponent with your fists to pull his attention up to his head, and then drop low and attack his legs. Although it can sometimes help to throw three or four punches before shooting in, as you can see in the sequence below it can also be accomplished using a simple jab. If you look at the photos, you'll notice that instead of pulling my jab back into my stance and then shooting in, I keep my jab in my opponent's face as I drop my elevation. This obscures his vision, making it easier for me to penetrate in. Once I've closed the distance and wrapped my arms around the back of my opponent's legs, I do not drive him straight back. It's possible to score a takedown in this fashion, but it gives your opponent better ability to sprawl his legs back, and it will also usually land you in his guard. A much better tactic is to use a technique that is commonly referred to as "turning the corner." To accomplish this, you drive your opponent horizontally once you've closed off all space between your bodies. In addition to disrupting your opponent's balance, which limits his defenses, it will also often land you in side control, which is more favorable than landing in his guard.

Dave and I are in orthodox stances, searching for an opening to attack.

I throw a jab into Dave's face to momentarily blind him and pull his focus up to his head.

Keeping my left hand in Dave's face to obscure his vision, I push off my rear foot, step my left foot forward, and drop my level by bending at the knees. Notice how I keep my right arm elevated to protect myself from counterstrikes.

Driving off my rear foot, I position my head against the left side of Dave's body, wrap my hands around the backs of his knees, and drop my left knee toward the mat.

Keeping Dave's legs tight to my body using my hands, I drop my knee to the mat between his legs, slide my right foot forward and to the outside of his left leg, and lift my head upright.

Instead of continuing linearly, I lift Dave's left leg off the mat using my right hand, block his right leg using my left hand, and drive him horizontally using my head. Notice how the combination of these actions causes him to lose his balance and begin falling toward his right side.

Continuing with my previous actions, Dave collapses to his back. I come down on top of him, clear his legs, and obtain side control.

Greg Jackson

Front Kick to Double-Leg Takedown

In this sequence I demonstrate how to setup a double-leg takedown by throwing a front kick to your opponent's face. Although front kicks directed at your opponent's midsection or hip generally cause him to bend forward, a stern push kick to the face will usually straighten his posture, either by elevating his chin with the collision or causing him to lean back to avoid the strike. For obvious reasons, this makes it much more difficult for him to defend against your shot by sprawling. To capitalize on that opening, instead of retracing your leg back into your stance after the kick, you drop your foot straight down to the mat and position it between your opponet's legs. This puts you in a perfect position to drop your elevation, wrap your arms around the back of his legs, and complete the double-leg takedown. The key to success with this technique is committing to your kick. If you throw a half ass kick and your opponent is not intimiated, instead of leaning back, he will most likely counter with a strike of his own, such as a cross. With your body moving into him, there is a good chance you will go to sleep if he lands clean. The upside to this technique is that it is infrequently utilized in MMA competiton, which often allows you to catch your opponent off guard.

Donald and I are in orthodox stances, searching for an opening to attack.

To setup a double-leg takedown, I elevate my lead knee toward my chest and then throw a front kick to Donald's face. Although it is not super important that you land the kick, you must to commit to it to get your opponent to lean back and increase his elevation.

Having leaned back to avoid my front kick, Donald is now vulnerable to a double-leg takedown. To capitalize on that vulnerability, I drop my left foot between his legs and drop my level. Notice how I have kept both of my arms elevated to protect myself from any possible counterstrikes.

As I drop my left knee toward the mat between Donald's legs, I wrap my right arm around the back of his left leg and my left arm around the back of his right leg. From here, I will turn the corner as Fitch did in the previous sequence and complete the takedown.

Forrest Griffin

Jab - Cross to Body - Takedown

This is a good set up for the double-leg takedown because it's deceptive. Just as Fitch did in the previous sequence, I begin by throwing a jab into my opponent's face to blind him and pull his focus high. Next, I step my lead foot forward and drop elevation, just as I would when executing a shot. However, instead of shooting in, I rotate my hips and throw a cross to my opponent's body. After landing the shot, your opponent will often assume that you've given up on the takedown and are content with striking. He'll expect you to increase your elevation and throw another strike to his head, but instead you keep your elevation low, step your rear foot between his legs, and wrap your arms around the backs of his knees to complete the double-leg takedown.

Lance and I are in orthodox stances, searching for an opening to attack.

I step my lead foot forward and throw a jab at Lance's face, pulling his focus high and momentarily blinding him.

I pull my left arm back into my stance, step my left leg forward, drop my elevation by bending at the knees, rotate my hips in a counterclockwise direction, and throw a cross at Lance's midsection. The instant I dropped my level he prepared for me to shoot, but now that I have thrown a strike, he expects me to rise back up and throw another strike.

Instead of increasing my elevation, I step my right foot between Lance's legs and move my right arm toward the back of his left leg.

I hook my right hand around the back of Lance's left knee and my left hand around the back of his right knee. From here, I can complete the double-leg takedown.

Forrest Griffin

Step-Out Hook - Shoot for Takedown

In this sequence I set up a double-leg takedown off a lead hook, but instead of throwing the hook directly from my stance, I throw it while stepping my rear leg to the outside of my opponent's lead leg. This gives me a dominant angle of attack and allows me to shoot on my opponent's legs from the side, making it a lot more difficult for him to defend against my takedown by sprawling. Once I've closed the distance and wrapped up his legs, I complete the takedown.

Lance and I are in orthodox stances, searching for an opening to attack.

To set up a double-leg takedown, I step my rear foot forward and to the outside of Lance's lead leg. At the same time, I throw a lead hook into his face to momentarily blind him and pull his focus high.

Before Lance can square his hips with mine and eliminate my dominant angle, I step my left foot forward and plant it between his legs. At the same time, I drop my level by bending my knees.

4

I drive into Lance so that my head is positioned on his left side and wrap my hands around the backs of his knees.

5

I pull Lance's left leg into me using my right hand, circle my body around him in a clockwise direction, and drive my left shoulder into his midsection. With his left leg pulled out from underneath him and my weight driving his body in the direction of his missing leg, he has no choice but to collapse toward his back.

6

As Lance collapses to his back, I come down on top of him and maintain control of his legs. From here, I will immediately work to pass his guard into side control

Forrest Griffin

Overhand - Shoot Double-Leg - Lift

In this sequence I demonstrate how to set up a double-leg takedown off an overhand right. The nice part about this combination is that the movement involved in the overhand right is very similar to the movement involved in the takedown, allowing you to blend them seamlessly. With the strike and takedown being back to back, your opponent must choose one to defend against. If he keeps his elevation high and blocks the overhand, you will most likely score the takedown. If he drops his level to block the takedown, you will most likely land with the overhand right. However, your opponent can defend against both techniques by backing up, which can leave you in a very compromising position. Therefore, I recommend using this technique when your opponent is backed up against the fence and doesn't have the ability to retreat.

Lance and I are in orthodox stances, searching for an opening to attack.

I step my left foot forward and to the outside of Lance's right foot, come up onto the ball of my right foot, rotate my hips in a counterclockwise direction, and throw an overhand right, which follows a similar path to a swimmer's freestyle stroke. Notice how I dipped my head and moved it away from my centerline to avoid his counterstrikes. While this is important, you do not want to dip your head too far—you must keep your eyes on your target.

Lance used his left arm to block my overhand right. With his elevation still erect, I use the momentum of my strike to transition into a double-leg takedown. I accomplish this by stepping my right foot forward and between his legs and wrapping my arms around the backs of his knees.

I step my left foot forward, increase my elevation, and lift Lance off the mat. From here, I can complete the takedown a number of different ways.

Shawn Tompkins

Cross - Lead Hook - Rear Hook - Lead Hook - Shoot

This is a combination that I have all my wrestlers practice. To begin, you throw a cross to force your opponent to lean backward, follow up with a lead hook to the side of his jaw to get him to lean back even more, and then drop your elevation. When your opponent sees your head go down, he will most likely think you are shooting in for a takedown and prepare to sprawl, but instead of shooting in, you throw a powerful cross to his body. With your opponent now focused on his midsection and legs, you pop back up to your fighting stance and throw another lead hook. Your opponent will suddenly realize the urgency of protecting his head and pull his focus high, and that's when you drop your level again. Having just dropped your level and thrown a punch, your opponent will expect that you are doing the exact same thing. However, instead of throwing a punch, this time you shoot in for a double-leg takedown. By going up and then down several times, you build your opponent's confidence that you aren't going to shoot, thereby making it much easier to score the takedown. The combination works best when the cage wall is about five feet behind your opponent. The cross and hook knocks him backward, you hit the body, and when you come back up for the second hook your opponent is still on his heels. With the cage just a couple of feet behind him now, you shoot in, bounce him off the chain link, secure the double-leg, and then dump him on his head. Mac Danzig, being a phenomenal wrestler, uses this technique and others like it all the time with great success.

Junie and I are in orthodox stances, searching for an opening to attack.

I rotate my hips in a counterclockwise direction, come up onto the ball of my right foot, and throw a cross at Junie's chin.

Rotating my hips in a clockwise direction, I plant my right foot on the mat, come up onto the ball of my left foot, and begin throwing a left hook.

I land a left hook to the side of Junie's jaw.

With my hips now spring-loaded, I drop my level by bending at the knees.

Rotating my hips in a counterclockwise direction again, I keep my left foot planted on the mat and come up onto the ball of my right foot. Notice how although my elevation is low, my back is still straight.

Continuing to rotate my hips in a counterclockwise direction, I land a right cross to Junie's midsection.

I increase my elevation, plant my right foot on the mat, come up onto the ball of my left foot, rotate my hips in a clockwise direction, and throw a lead left hook toward the left side of Junie's jaw.

I land a left hook to Junie's jaw.

I again drop my elevation by bending at the knees.

Instead of throwing another right cross, I drive forward off my right foot and reach my arms toward the backs of Junie's legs.

I step my right foot between Junie's legs and wrap my arms around the backs of his knees. From here, I can complete the double-leg takedown.

Jon Fitch

Lead Hook - Single-Leg - Run the Pipe

In this sequence I demonstrate how to set up a single-leg takedown off a lead hook. If you look at the photos below, you'll notice that my hips get spring-loaded when I throw the lead hook. If my goal was to keep the fight standing, I could use that coiled energy to unleash a right-handed strike, but since I want to bring the fight to the mat, I use it to snap my lead foot forward and to the outside of my opponent's lead leg. Once accomplished, it becomes very easy for me to wrap my rear hand around the outside of his lead leg. To establish an even better trap on his lead leg, I clasp my hands together on the inside of his lead knee. This allows me to pull his leg up to my chest and secure the single-leg position. There are many takedowns that can be executed from the single-leg position, but perhaps the most common is a technique called "running the pipe." All it entails is forcing your opponent's body in the direction of his missing leg, which can be accomplished by stepping your lead foot backward and your rear foot forward and driving your opponent's body circularly using your head.

Dave and I are in orthodox stances, searching for an opening to attack.

Planting my right foot on the mat and coming up onto the ball of my left foot, I throw a lead left hook to the side of Dave's jaw.

With my hips now spring-loaded, I unleash that energy by stepping my right foot forward and to the outside of Dave's left leg. At the same time, I hook my right hand around the outside of his left leg. It is important to notice that I have positioned my head in the center of his chest.

I grab my right wrist using my left hand and then pull Dave's leg up to my chest, establishing the single-leg position.

I slide my left foot forward along a circular path. Next, I slide my right foot backward along a circular path. Once accomplished, I drive Dave's body toward his missing leg using my head. Notice how the combination of these actions causes him to lose balance and fall toward the mat.

As Dave lands on his back, I maintain control of his left leg to prevent him from scrambling and quickly popping back up to his feet. From here, I can remain standing and strike or circle over his leg to his left side and establish side control.

Jon Fitch

Failed Single-Leg to Body Dump

In this sequence I demonstrate how to shoot in for an outside single-leg just as I did in the previous sequence, but as you obtain control of your opponent's lead leg, he drives your head toward the mat using his hand. With your ass positioned above your head, there is no way you can lift his leg to your chest and complete the single-leg takedown. Instead of continuing for the single-leg, drive your body forward and attempt to execute a double-leg takedown by securing control of your opponent's rear leg as well. Sometimes you will be successful with the reshoot double, and other times your opponent will prevent you from seizing control of his rear leg by sprawling his legs backward. As you will learn below, if the latter occurs, all is not lost. If you managed to penetrate deep enough to get your head positioned between your opponent's legs, you will usually have the leverage needed to lift his body up onto your shoulders. Once accomplished, you can dump him over to one side, drop your weight down on top of him, and establish the side control position.

Dave and I are in orthodox stances, searching for an opening to attack.

I rotate my hips in a counterclockwise direction, come up onto the ball of my right foot, and throw a right cross at Dave's chin.

I move my right leg forward and drop my knee to the outside of Dave's left leg. At the same time, I wrap my right arm around the outside of his left leg and clasp my hands together.

Before I can pull Dave's left leg up to my chest and establish the single-leg position, he counters by sprawling his legs back, dropping his weight down onto my back, and driving my head downward using his right hand. Although it will be difficult for me to complete the takedown by running the pipe from this position, it is important to notice that I still have my right hand hooked around the back of his left knee.

Pulling Dave's left leg toward me using my right hand, I position my head between his legs, plant my left hand on the mat, and then sit up. Notice how this loads his weight onto my back.

6

Sitting all the way up, I place my left hand on Dave's right knee.

7

With my right hand still hooked around the back of Dave's left knee, I push his right leg over my head using my left hand. Notice how this dumps his body toward my right side.

8

As I dump Dave over to his back, I immediately drop my right shoulder into his midsection to prevent him from scrambling and escaping the side control position.

9

To secure side control, I wrap my right arm around the back of Dave's head, wrap my left arm around the outside of his left leg, plant my torso on his torso, and position my left knee against his left hip. From here, I can immediately begin my ground attack.

STRIKING TO THE SINGLE-LEG

THE ULTIMATE MIXED MARTIAL ARTIST

Jon Fitch

Evade Jab to Double-Leg Takedown

In this sequence I demonstrate how to evade your opponent's jab by dropping your elevation and executing an outside slip, and then shoot underneath his extended arm and execute a double-leg takedown. Setting up takedowns by countering your opponent's strikes is sometimes even more effective than setting up takedowns with strikes of your own because his body is moving toward you. In order for him to effectively defend against your takedown, he must pull his arm back into his body and reestablish his fighting stance before you can secure control of his legs, and this is hard to manage when committed to a strike. The key to success with this technique is putting your initial focus into eluding your opponent's strike. If you get ahead of yourself and shoot in for his legs prematurely, there is a good chance your opponent will redirect his punch and club you in the face. It is also important to be certain your opponent is committing to the punch. A lot of times fighters will fake a strike to get you to drop your elevation, and then throw an alternate strike such as a knee to the face as you shoot in.

Dave and I are in orthodox stances, searching for an opening to attack.

Dave throws a jab at my face. To slip his punch, I rotate my shoulders slightly in a clockwise direction, drop my level by bending my knees, and move my head toward my right. Notice how my actions cause his fist to move past the left side of my head.

Instead of increasing my elevation after slipping Dave's jab, I drive forward, drop my left knee between his legs, and wrap my arms around the backs of his knees. With Dave's arm extended forward with his punch, he is unable to sprawl and defend against my shot.

I slide my right foot in a counterclockwise direction across the mat, pull Dave's right leg toward me using my left hand, lift his left leg using my right hand, and drive him toward my left using my head. Notice how by cutting the corner in this fashion I have shattered his base and balance.

As Dave collapses to his back, I drive my left shoulder into his midsection to assume side control and prevent him from scrambling back to his feet.

To secure side control, I wrap my left hand around the back of Dave's head, hook my right arm around the outside of his right hip, and drop my torso down on top of his.

Jon Fitch

Evade Cross to Single-Leg Takedown

In this sequence my opponent and I are in the same fighting stance, and he throws a cross at my face. As I evade his strike by dropping my elevation, I step my rear leg forward and to the outside of his lead leg. This puts me in a perfect position to wrap my arms around his lead leg and pull it up to my chest, securing the single-leg position. Once accomplished, I take him to the mat by running the pipe, which was demonstrated in an earlier sequence.

Dave and I are in orthodox stances, searching for an opening to attack.

Dave comes up onto the ball of his right foot and throws a cross toward my face. To evade his punch and set up a takedown at the same time, I step my right foot forward and to the outside of his lead leg and drop my elevation.

As Dave's cross sails past my head, I wrap my right arm around the outside of his left leg, grab my right wrist with my left hand, and position my head on the right side of his body.

I establish the single-leg position by stepping my left foot forward and pulling Dave's left leg up to my chest.

To run the pipe and get the takedown, I slide my right foot back and drive Dave toward his missing leg using my head.

As Dave lands on his back, I have the option of moving to the outside of his body and securing side control as demonstrated in previous sequences or remain standing and launching a ground-and-pound attack as shown here.

Anderson Silva

Hand Stop to Knee Strike

When you and your opponent are in opposite fighting stances, your lead leg is positioned close to his lead arm, making it easy for him to drop his level and shoot in for a single-leg takedown. Although there are many ways to counter his shot, the method shown here is by far the simplest because you use your first line of defense, which are your hands. The most critical part of this technique is timing. The instant your opponent drops his level and shoots in, place your hands on his shoulders to stop his forward momentum and shoot your lead leg back to prevent him from latching on to it. When done correctly, it leaves your opponent kneeling in front of you. If you are competing in Japan where knees to the face of a grounded opponent are legal, you have a perfect opportunity to drive your rear knee straight forward and into your opponent's jaw. If you are competing in events where kneeing a downed opponent is illegal, you can simply back away.

Feijao is in an orthodox stance, and I'm in a southpaw stance. Both of us are looking for an opening to attack.

Feijao throws his left hand forward to pull my focus high, alerting me to the fact that he is most likely trying to set up a takedown.

As Feijao drops his level and begins shooting forward for my lead leg, I sink my hips back.

Continuing to sink my hips back, I step my right foot behind me to remove it from Feijao's reach and place my hands on his shoulders to halt his forward momentum.

Having created distance between our bodies, I drive my right knee into Feijao's face before he can reshoot or come back up to his feet.

Anderson Silva

Double Underhooks to Knee

This sequence depicts the same scenario as the last—you and your opponent are in opposite fighting stances, and he shoots in to obtain control of your lead leg. With your opponent having timed his shot, you are unable to execute the previous technique and employ your first line of defense. As a result, you employ your second line of defense, which are your arms. To accomplish this, you reach your arms underneath your opponent's arms as he shoots forward, establishing double underhooks. Once accomplished, you use your underhooks to pull his body upright and destroy his chances of reaching your legs. Before your opponent can increase his level and reestablish his fighting stance, you drive your rear knee into his midsection.

Feijao is in an orthodox stance, and I'm in a southpaw stance. Both of us are searching for an opening to attack.

Feijao drops his level to shoot in for a single-leg takedown.

As Feijao steps his left foot to the outside of my right foot and reaches for my lead leg, I drop my right hand.

I hook my right hand underneath Feijao's left arm and hook my left hand underneath his right arm. Next, I use my double underhooks to pull his body upward, making it very difficult for him to obtain control of my lead leg.

Before Feijao can reshoot or increase his elevation, I drive my left knee upward into his face.

Jab - Cross - Opponent Shoots - Defend with Knee

When you are punishing a wrestler with strikes, you can pretty much guarantee that at some point he is going to attempt to drop underneath your punches and shoot in for a takedown. As long as you are not leaning dramatically forward on your punches or overextending your arms, you will often have enough time to pull your arm back into your stance and deliver a knee to your opponent's face as he comes forward. However, even when you manage to stop your opponent's initial shot with your knee, there are a lot of fighters who are masters at reshooting off a missed shot. For this reason, recovery is very important. You want to immediately pull your leg back into your stance and reestablish your base. Should your opponent shoot in for a second time, this gives you the ability to land another knee to his face as his body rockets forward.

Junie and I are in orthodox stances, searching for an opening to attack.

I throw a jab at Junie's face.

Rotating my hips in a counterclockwise direction, I pull my left arm back into my body and prepare to throw a cross.

Coming up onto the ball of my right foot, I throw a cross at Junie's chin.

In an attempt to evade my barrage, Junie drops his level to shoot in for a takedown. To counter, I throw my right knee into his jaw.

As Junie gets knocked backward from my strike, I pull my right leg back and plant my foot on the mat.

7) Not wanting to take more abuse on his feet, Junie keeps his elevation low, shifts his weight onto his lead leg, and again shoots in for a takedown. To counter, I begin to throw another right knee strike toward his face.

8) As Junie reshoots, he eats another right knee to the face.

Shawn Tompkins

Opponent Shoots - Uppercut - Hook - Pivot - Cross

In this sequence I demonstrate another way to utilize strikes to defend against your opponent's double-leg takedown attempt. The instant you see him drop his level, rotate toward your rear leg, lower your elevation, and then unleash an uppercut to his advancing jaw. This lifts his chin, creating an opportunity to immediately follow up with a lead hook to the side of his face. If you're up against a good wrestler who desperately wants to take the fight to the ground, chances are he will reshoot after these two strikes. To prevent him from scoring a takedown, immediately pivot on your lead foot and circle your rear leg to the outside of his body. When done quickly, your opponent will shoot right past your body. With nothing to grab a hold of, he will most likely fall forward, creating a perfect opportunity for you to land a cross to the back of his ear.

Junie and I are in orthodox stances, searching for an opening to attack.

Junie drops his level, alerting me to the fact that he might be preparing to shoot in for a takedown. To prepare my defense, I rotate my body in a clockwise direction, spring-loading my hips and right hand.

As Junie penetrates in for a takedown, I begin dropping my right hand.

Rotating my hips in a counterclockwise direction, I come up onto the ball of my right foot, drop my right hand, and then deliver a rear uppercut to Junie's jaw, halting his forward momentum and takedown attempt.

Determined to get the takedown, Junie shifts his weight back onto his lead leg and continues to penetrate in. To defend against his shot, I begin rotating my hips in a clockwise direction and throw a lead hook toward the side of his head.

Before Junie can gain control of my legs, I land a lead hook to the side of his head. Notice how this forces his body to move toward his left, making it difficult for him to obtain control of my legs.

To ensure Junie doesn't obtain control of my legs, I pivot on my left foot and slide my right foot in a clockwise direction across the mat. This puts my body off to his side, not only making it difficult for him to complete the takedown, but also giving me a dominant angle of attack.

As Junie's shot carries him forward into open air, I rotate my hips in a counterclockwise direction, come up onto the ball of my right foot, and throw a cross at the side of his head.

Sprawling off Knee Strike

In previous sequences Shawn Tompkins and Anderson Silva demonstrated how to block your opponent's shot and then counter with a knee strike. Although they are all excellent techniques, it is important to prepare yourself for the likely chance that your opponent will wrap his arms around your knee and captures your leg. If he manages to obtain solid control of your leg, pull your knee up to his chest, and increase his elevation, he will have achieved the single-leg position. Later in the book we demonstrate multiple ways to escape the single-leg position, but the goal here is to avoid having to go through that process. If you feel your opponent wrapping his arms around your leg as you land the knee strike, you'll have a narrow window of opportunity to prevent him from obtaining solid control. To make use of that window, shoot your elevated leg behind you to strip your opponent's hands from your leg. Next, drop your body down on top of him and execute a sprawl by shooting your grounded leg behind you. The combination of these actions prevents your opponent from obtaining control of either of your legs. If you look at the photos below, you'll notice that when executing the sprawl I do not position my arms in front of my opponent's shoulders. Although this offers much better control, if you try to assume this dominant position after landing the knee strike, your opponent will have the time he needs to secure the single-leg position. With this particular technique, the primary goal is to escape your leg from your opponent's grasp and sprawl your body out on top of him as quickly as possible. Once you reach sprawl control, that's when you work on securing proper arm positioning.

Lance drops his elevation and shoots in for a takedown.

Before Lance can obtain control of my legs, I throw a right knee strike into his jaw.

Although I caused Lance damage with my right knee strike, he continues to drive his weight forward and wrap his arms around the back of my legs to complete a takedown.

Without hesitating, I drop my chest down onto Lance's upper back and shoot my right leg straight behind me.

I continue to sprawl by shooting my left leg behind me, dropping my weight down onto Lance's back, and driving my hips toward the mat. Notice how this forces Lance's head to the mat, making it very difficult for him to complete the takedown. From here, I can escape back to my feet or launch a ground attack.

Half Stock to Back

In this sequence I demonstrate how to stop your opponent's double-leg takedown by sprawling your legs back, hooking one arm around the front of his shoulder (a technique often referred to as a "half stock"), and dropping your hips to the mat. While it is possible to execute just as effective a defense by placing both of your arms in front of your opponent's shoulders (known as the "full stock"), the goal here is not simply to block your opponent's shot, but also to circle around behind him and take his back. By keeping one arm free, you can use your hand to drive your opponent's arm underneath his body, which prevents him from grabbing your body with his arm as you circle. If you look at the photos below, you'll notice that once I reach his side, I hook my arm over his back. This serves as a kind of seat belt, making it difficult for him to escape the position. However, instead of grabbing around his waist, I hook my hand around the inside of his thigh. This prevents him from grabbing a hold of my arm and then rolling me over to my back. When you stabilize the position in this fashion, you are in a much better position to begin dropping punches to your opponent's head.

As Neil drops his level and begins shooting in for a double-leg takedown, I immediately start dropping my level. However, it is important to note that I have kept my hands elevated to protect my head should he abandon the takedown and throw a cross or overhand right.

As Neil penetrates in for the takedown, I position my left arm in front of his right shoulder, dramatically impeding his forward momentum.

Before Neil can obtain control of my legs, I sprawl my legs back and drive my left hip toward the mat. With his forward momentum being halted by my left arm and his body being driven downward by my hips, he is unable to gain control of my legs. To set up my transition to his back, I place my right hand on his left triceps.

I drive Neil's left arm underneath his body using my right hand, feeding his arm to my left hand. Once I have a solid left grip on his arm, I will be free to circle around to his back.

Maintaining control of Neil's left arm using my left hand, I reach my right hand over his back and to the inside of his right leg. Next, I begin circling my body around him in a counterclockwise direction. Notice how with his left arm trapped, he is unable to grab my legs and prevent my transition.

Circling around to Neil's left side, I place my right knee on the mat, drive my right hip into his left hip, and pull my left arm back to punch. It is important to note that I still have my right hand hooked around the inside of his right thigh. This allows me to control his body, but at the same time makes it difficult for him to grab my arm and roll me over to my back.

Erin Toughill

Full Stock to Reverse Full Nelson

In the previous sequence I demonstrated how to block your opponent's double-leg takedown and circle around to his back utilizing a sprawl and a half stock. In this sequence I have the same primary goal of stopping my opponent's takedown, but instead of desiring to take his back, I want to flip him over to his back and catch him in a nasty neck crank. To accomplish this, I employ a full stock by placing both of my arms in front of his shoulders as he shoots in. Before he can obtain control of my hips, I sprawl my legs back, drive my weight down on top of him, and flatten his body out on the mat. From this position, it becomes very difficult for him to move. That lack of mobility allows me to use my hooks under his shoulders to flip him over to his back by simply turning my body. Still holding on to my initial hooks, my opponent's head gets trapped underneath my armpit as he lands on his backside, which makes applying the neck crank as easy as leaning my weight back into his head.

While in my fighting stance, Neil drops his level and shoots in for a double-leg takedown.

Before Neil can seize control of my legs, I employ a full stock by placing my arms in front of his shoulders and hooking my hands underneath his arms. Notice how this places his head in my left armpit.

As Neil continues to drive forward for the takedown, I sprawl my legs behind me and drive my left hip to the mat. My actions force his forward energy down into the mat, making it very difficult for him to reach my legs.

I hook my hands around Neil's back to keep his head trapped in my left armpit, come up onto my left knee, and then use my arms to force him over toward his back.

As I roll Neil over to his back, I begin scissoring my legs. Notice how I have kept his head trapped in my left armpit.

I scissor my legs by moving my left leg underneath my right leg and my right leg over my left leg. Once I have established a sturdy base, I keep my grips tight and arch backward, putting a tremendous amount of pressure on Neil's neck.

Erin Toughill

Collar Tie Get Up

In this sequence, my opponent manages to close the distance between us, seize control of my legs, and put me on my back by executing a double-leg takedown. Due to the nature of most double-leg takedowns, his legs land on one side of my body and his head on the other. Before he can smother me and improve his positioning, I immediately turn onto my side and place my far elbow on the mat. At the same time, I secure a collar tie with my near arm, planting my elbow in front of his shoulder. My opponent's goal is to scoot his hips up my body to obtain a more dominant hold, but with my elbow on his shoulder, I am able to temporarily keep him at bay. I use that small window of opportunity to push his head onto the same side of my body as his legs using my collar tie, and then drive his head downward into the mat. The combination of these actions reduces the control he has over my body, allowing me to slip my legs out from underneath him and escape back to my feet. However, it is important when making this escape not to try to push your opponent away from you, because this will be an impossible feat due to your minimal leverage. Instead, you want to push your body away from your opponent. To increase your success with this technique, it is important to secure your collar tie and reposition your opponent's head the instant he completes the takedown. If you delay, he will creep his hips up your body and secure a much more dominant hold.

Neil has shot in and secured control of my legs.

Before I can defend against his takedown, Neil hefts me off the canvas and executes his double-leg.

The instant I land on my back, I turn toward my right side and place my left hand on right side of Neil's head.

4

I turn onto my right side, place my right elbow on the mat, and secure a left collar tie. With my left elbow digging into Neil's right shoulder, he has a difficult time moving his weight into me. I use this opportunity to drive his head to the right side of my body and then down into the mat.

5

My previous actions have dramatically reduced Neil's control over my body. Keeping his head pinned to the mat using my left collar tie, I pull my right leg out from underneath his body and post my knee on the mat.

6

I straighten my right arm on the mat and pop up to my feet. To prevent Neil from reshooting for a double-leg, I keep his head pinned to the mat using my left hand.

7

As I back away from Neil, I keep my right hand on his head to hinder him from shooting in for another takedown.

Jon Fitch

Sprawl off Opposite Stance

Although the majority of fighters will shoot in for a single-leg takedown when in opposite fighting stances, there are fighters who break this rule and shoot in for a double-leg. In this sequence, I demonstrate how to defend against this takedown using a sprawl. As your opponent shoots in, place your rear hand on top of his head and drive it downward. This pushes his forward momentum into the mat, making it very difficult for him to reach your back leg. At the same time, circle your rear leg away from his reaching arms to make it even more difficult for him to wrap his hands around the backs of your knees. Once both tasks are accomplished, slide your near hand underneath your opponent's body, turn back into him, and drop your chest down onto his back. This puts you in sprawl control and gives you a number of options. You can use your dominant positioning to stand back up as demonstrated below, or you can use your positioning to strike, which is demonstrated in the next sequence.

Dave is in a southpaw stance, and I'm in an orthodox stance. Both of us are searching for an opening to attack.

Dave drops his level and wraps his right arm around the back of my left leg, working for a takedown.

Before Dave can wrap his left arm around the back of my right leg, I sprawl my left leg out toward my left side, drive my left side down into his upper back, and place my right hand on the top of his head.

4

Continuing to drop my left hip toward the mat, I drive Dave's face downward using my right hand, hindering his ability to continue to shoot forward for the takedown.

5

Now that I've stopped Dave's shot, I transition to sprawl control by sprawling my right leg behind me and dropping my chest down onto his upper back.

6

I place my hands on Dave's knees to prevent him from driving forward again as I transition to the standing position.

7

I post on my left knee and place my left hand on the back of Dave's neck to keep his head pinned to the mat. This prevents him from shooting forward and seizing control of my legs as I stand.

Jon Fitch

Striking from Sprawl Control

In this sequence I demonstrate some of your various options for striking from sprawl control. If you look at the photos below, you'll notice that I angle my body off to the side of my opponent before unleashing with punches. This is very important because in order to obtain a position from which to strike, you must release some of the pressure off your opponent's back, which in turn gives him the ability to elevate his head. If he can elevate his head enough, it is possible for him to once again drive forward in an attempt to obtain control of your legs and complete a takedown. By angling your body off to his side, it makes it very difficult for him to accomplish this goal. It is also important to notice that I obtain two different positions in the sequence below. In the first position, I simply angle off to the side and begin pounding on my opponent's head. While this method allows you to throw quick strikes, it doesn't offer optimal control. In the second position, I reach my hand over my opponent's back and underneath his body, obtaining control of his far wrist. While this takes a little more time to set up, it offers much better control. By eliminating one of your opponent's arms from the equation, he is unable to complete takedowns. He also can't roll into your guard, which is a common escape route from this position.

I've established sprawl control on Dave.

To establish a safe position from which to strike, I circle in a clockwise direction around Dave's body, elevate my right hip, drive my left hip down into his right shoulder, and pull my right arm back.

I throw a right punch at the left side of Dave's face

To transition to an even safer position from which to strike, I slide my right foot across the mat in a clockwise direction, and slide my left knee toward my right foot. Notice how this causes Dave's right arm to slide off of my left leg. At the same time, I wrap my left arm over his back and underneath his body.

I grab Dave's left wrist with my left hand, which locks him in place and prevents him from pulling guard. Now positioned on the side of his body, I draw my right hand back to strike.

I land a right punch to the right side of Dave's head.

Block Overhand to Takedown Defense

Most fighters nowadays know better than to shoot blindly in for a takedown. To set up their shot, they will often throw a jab, hook, or an overhand as they drop their level and penetrate in for your legs. When your opponent choses to utilize an overhand, the technique demonstrated below is an excellent option to prevent him from both landing his punch and scoring a takedown. The technique itself is rather simple--all you do is block the overhand and then step your lead leg behind you. The key to being successful with it is positioning your rear arm in front of the shoulder of your opponent's punching arm. This prevents him from closing the distance and seizing control of your legs as he follows through with his strike. Once you have effectively blocked his attack, you can disengage and immediately get your offense going. I strongly suggest practicing this technique because the overhand to double-leg is one of the most common striking to takedown combinations in MMA.

Feijao is in an orthodox stance, and I am in a southpaw stance. Both of us are searching for an opening to attack.

Feijao steps his lead foot forward, shifts his weight onto his lead leg, and throws an oeverhand right. Immediataly I elevate both arms to block his strike.

I reach my right hand forward and place it in front of Feijao's right shoulder. At the same time, I catch his right forearm using my left arm.

4

As Feijao drops his elevation to shoot in for a takedown, I keep my right hand on his right shoulder.

5

Holding Feijao at bay using my right hand, I step my lead leg behind me.

6

Having shot my lead leg out of Feijao's reach, I drop down to my right knee and hold him at bay using my right hand. Once I have stopped all his forward momentum, I can work back to my feet.

Anderson Silva

DEFENDING THE DOUBLE-LEG

OPPOSITE STANCE

Defending Double-Leg with Sprawl and Choke

In this sequence my opponent shoots in for a double-leg takedown with his head positioned to the inside of my body, which happens from time to time. To increase the number of defenses at my disposal, I immediately place my hands on his head and move it to the outside of my body. This allows me to sprawl my legs away from him and drop my chest onto his back. Oftentimes, this is enough to get my opponent to abandon his shot. However, in the sequence below my opponent is desperate for the takedown and keeps his arms wrapped around the back of my legs. With his arms stretched away from his body, I have the space I need to trap his head and arm by establishing a figure-four lock. To tighten the lock and limit his defenses, I roll over my shoulder, across my back, and onto my side, pulling him with me. Once accomplished, I sever the blood flow to his brain by pinching my elbows together, forcing him to tap in submission. The key to being successful with this technique is being tight and explosive with your roll. If you relax your grips or execute a sloppy roll, your opponent will most likely escape your hold and the submission.

My opponent has shot in for a double-leg takedown and positioned his head to the inside of my body.

To increase my defensive options, I place cup my right hand on the right side of my opponent's face and begin moving his head toward the outside of my body.

As I move my opponent's head toward the outside of my body, I grab his right wrist with my left hand.

I reach my right hand toward the left side of my opponent's head.

Bending at the waist, I hook my right arm around the left side of my opponent's head and across his neck.

I drive my chest down into my opponent's upper back and break his left grip by sprawling my right leg behind me.

I sprawl my legs back and drop my chest down onto my opponent's upper back. At the same time, I shoot my left arm forward.

I grab my left biceps with my right hand, and then wrap my left hand over my opponent's back. This gives me a figure-four grip. It is important to notice that my left arm is positioned to the outside of my opponent's right arm.

Keeping my figure-four grip locked tight, I roll over onto my left shoulder.

I roll over onto my back, pulling my opponent with me.

As I roll toward my right side, my opponent is forced onto his back. Notice how I still have the figure-four locked tight, choking my opponent.

To finish the choke, I squeeze my elbows together and walk my lower body toward my opponent in a clockwise direction. With the blood flow severed to his brain, he has no choice but to tap.

Karo Parisyan

Countering Double-Leg with Uchi-Mata

In this sequence you and your opponent are in opposite stances and he shoots in to execute an outside leg trip, which is a variation of a double-leg. To turn the tables in your favor, you obtain control of his upper body, rotate so your back is facing his chest, and then execute a judo technique called Uchi-Mata by dropping your head and elevating your leg between your opponent's legs. Although your leverage isn't great on this technique because your opponent's body is so low, when done properly, you'll usually be able to lift his body slightly off the mat and dump him to his back. It is important to mention that although my opponent in the sequence below is executing an outside leg trip, as long as you can get your lead leg between your opponent's legs, this technique is just as effective for defending against the regular double-leg takedown and single-leg takedown.

I'm squared off with Neil, looking for an opening to attack.

Before I can launch my attack, Neil drops his elevation and begins shooting in for a takedown. As he closes the distance, he drives his head underneath my right arm and begins wrapping both of his arms around my hips.

Locking his hands together in the small of my back, Neil continues to drive forward for the takedown. In an attempt to take me down with an outside leg trip, Neil hooks his left leg around the outside of my right leg.

As Neil continues to drive forward, he hooks his left leg all the way around the back of my right leg. Immediately I rotate my body in a counterclockwise direction, latch on to his right triceps with my left hand, reach my right arm around the back of his head, and grab his upper left lat muscle where it meets his armpit with my right hand. Next, I hop my left foot to the outside of Neil's left knee. Not only does this turn my back to my opponent, but it also positions my hips to the outside of my trapped leg. If you keep your hips to the inside of your trapped leg, you will be unable to use your opponent's forward momentum against him and fail with the throw.

Continuing to corkscrew my body in a counterclockwise direction, I drive my right leg backward into Neil's left hip and pull on his left lat with my right hand. Having successfully used Neil's forward momentum against him, he gets tossed over to his back.

To secure the mount position, I sit down on Neil's side, hook my right leg underneath his left leg, and posture up. From here, I can start dropping punches and elbows or immediately begin working for a submission.

Anderson Silva

Hand Fight Defense for Single-Leg

This is a very basic technique for escaping the single-leg position. If your opponent has your right leg captured, you wrap your right hand around the back of his neck to secure a collar tie and grab his near wrist using your left hand. Using your left grip, you force his wrist downward to break his clasped hands apart. The instant you accomplish this, his control of your captured leg weakens significantly, allowing you to drive your foot back down to the mat. This gives you a couple of options. If your goal is to create separation, you can simply back away. If your goal is to make your opponent pay for his takedown attempt, you can use your head and wrist control to off-balance your opponent and then land a knee strike to his face, which is demonstrated below.

Feijao is in an orthodox stance, and I'm in a southpaw stance. Both of us are searching for an opening to attack.

Feijao drops his level and shoots in for my lead leg.

Feijao manages to capture my lead leg and pull it up to his chest, securing the single-leg position. Immediately I wrap my left hand around the back of his head, securing a collar tie.

Keeping my right hand wrapped around the back of Feijao's head, I grab his right wrist with my left hand.

I separate Feijao's grip using my left hand by forcing his right arm toward the outside of his body. Once his grip is broken, I immediately drop my right foot toward the mat.

I drop my right foot to the mat and then use my right collar tie and left wrist grip to maintain control of his body.

I drive Feijao's right arm away from his body using my left hand. At the same time, I use my right collar tie to pull his body in a clockwise direction, disrupting his balance.

I continue to disrupt Feijao's balance by forcing his body in a clockwise direction using my grips.

With Feijao's base destroyed, I step back, release control of his right wrist, secure the Muay Thai clinch by clasping my hands together behind his head, and then pull his head downward.

I drive my right knee up into Feijao's face.

Jon Fitch

Defending Single-Leg with Sprawl

In the previous sequence Anderson demonstrated how to escape the single-leg position. In this sequence, I demonstrate how to prevent your opponent from obtaining the single-leg position by driving his head down and sprawling your legs back when he shoots in. The technique lands you in sprawl control, which gives you a numerous options. If your goal is to keep the fight standing, you can pop back up to your feet. If your goal is to strike your opponent on the mat, you can establish one of the dominant sprawl control positions I demonstrated earlier and begin your ground and pound.

Dave and I are in orthodox stances, searching for an opening to attack.

Dave throws an overhand right. To block his strike, I reach my left hand behind my ear and press my forearm against the side of my head.

Immediately after throwing the overhand right, Dave drops his elevation, steps his right leg forward, and wraps his right arm around the outside of my left leg.

Dave clasps his hands together, but before he can pull my leg up to his chest, I defend his takedown by sprawling my left leg out toward my left side, dropping my left shoulder down into his back, and pushing his head toward the mat using my right hand. Notice how my actions make it nearly impossible for him to pull my leg up to his chest and secure the single-leg position.

To continue with my defense, I sprawl my left leg back, drop my hips toward the mat, and drive my chest into Dave's upper back.

I establish sprawl control as Dave drops down to all fours.

Anderson Silva

Knee Pick Single

It's always best to defend against your opponent's takedowns before he can gain control of your legs, but that isn't always possible. In this sequence my opponent manages to penetrate in and gain control of my lead leg. I have the option of repositioning his head to the outside of my body to increase my defensive options, but instead I blade my body so that my side is turned into him. At the same time, I slide my near arm between our bodies to create separation between us. This is key—without separation, this technique won't work. Once accomplished, the next step is to trap both of his legs in place to prevent him from stepping. To accomplish this, I hook my near leg around his near leg and slide my near arm down his body and hook it around the inside of his rear leg. To complete the takedown, I drop my hips below my opponent's hips and then drive his body circularly using my head. Unable to step in any direction to regain his balance due to my grips, he collapses to the mat. The two keys to success with this technique are creating enough space to trap your opponent's legs and dropping your hips below his hips. Even if you have both of his legs trapped, you won't have the leverage needed to drive him over to his back if you fail to drop your hips.

My opponent has shot in and secured control of my lead leg. Instead of forcing his head to the outside of my body, I turn sideways and dig my left arm between our bodies.

Creating separation between our bodies using my left arm, I hook my left leg around the inside of his right leg.

I drop down to my left knee and reach my left arm to the inside of my opponent's left arm.

I hook my left arm around the inside of my opponent's left leg.

Hooking my left hand around my opponent's left calf, I force him in a counterclockwise direction using my head and body. With my left leg hooked around his right leg and my left hand blocking his left leg, he is unable to step and regain his balance. As a result, he begins falling toward the mat.

As my opponent lands on his back, I scoop my left arm underneath his left leg.

I circle my arm to force my opponent's left leg away from his body. Notice how this gives me an unobstructed path to side control.

I clear my opponent's left leg and then drop my left hand on the mat next to his right hip.

I circle my body, placing my left knee in the small of my opponent's back, my right knee by his left shoulder, and my right hand above his head.

Having established side control, I elevate my right elbow to begin my ground-and-pound assault.

Anderson Silva

Defending against Single-Leg with Choke

There are numerous ways to escape the single-leg position, but sometimes those escapes are hard to manage when up against an experienced wrestler familiar with single-leg defense. If all your escape options fail, it is important to remember that there are also a number of submissions available from the position. In this particular technique, you capitalize on the fact that both of your opponent's arms are tied up with your lead leg and attack his neck with a chokehold. When applied correctly, you sever blood flow to your opponent's brain. To prevent from blacking out, your opponent must attack your hold using his hands, which requires him to release control of your captured leg. Even if your opponent manages to defend against the submission, you will still have escaped a very compromising position.

Feijao has captured my right leg and established the single-leg position.

Immediately I place my left hand on the top of Feijao's head to prevent him from posturing and press my right biceps against the left side of his neck.

I position the crook of my right arm around the front of Feijao's neck and then wrap my forearm around the right side of his neck.

I grab my left biceps with my right hand and then wrap my left hand over Feijao's back, securing a reverse rear naked choke. In order to defend against the submission, he must first release control of my right leg.

Anderson Silva

Countering Single-Leg with Scissor to Kneebar

In this sequence I demonstrate how to use a leg scissor to counter your opponent's single-leg takedown with a takedown of your own. The downside is that the takedown puts you on your back as well, which is far from optimal from a wrestling standpoint. You have the option of scrambling and establishing the top position, but I prefer to use my positioning to secure a kneebar submission. With my opponent's lead leg trapped between my legs as I land, applying the knee bar is as simple as grabbing his lower leg with my arms and extending my hips into his knee, hyperextending his leg.

My opponent is in an orthodox stance, and I'm in a southpaw stance. Both of us are searching for an opening to attack.

My opponent shoots in and secures control of my lead leg.

In order to pull off the leg scissor, I need to create separation between our bodies. I accomplish this by stepping back with my rear leg and pushing off my opponent's shoulder using my lead hand.

Now that I've created separation, I drop my level and step my lead foot deep between my opponent's legs. Notice how I still have my hand wrapped over his back.

I place my left hand on the mat near my left foot.

With my right arm hooked over my opponent's back, I shoot my left leg behind his left leg. Next, I hook my right leg around the inside of his upper left thigh.

Maintaining my balance using my arms, I rotate toward my back and scissor my legs. Notice how this chops my opponent's left leg out from underneath him and causes him to fall toward the mat.

Continuing to scissor my legs, my opponent gets forced toward his back. To ensure he goes over, I cup my right hand in his right armpit and use that control to pull his body downward.

As my opponent lands on his back, I hook my left foot in the crook of his right leg to keep his knees separated. This will make it more difficult for him to scramble out of the position. At the same time, I hook my left arm underneath his left leg.

I trap my opponent's left leg by sliding my right foot underneath my left leg. Next, I lean back and pull his left leg to my chest using my left arm.

Straightening my left leg to keep my opponent's knees separated, I trap his left leg flush with my chest using both of my arms. To apply the kneebar submission, I elevate my hips into his leg, hyperextending his knee.

Anderson Silva

Toehold Drive

Sometimes your opponent will become so focused on scoring a takedown that he forgets the weapons that you have in your arsenal, such as strikes and submissions. In this sequence my opponent shoots in and latches on to my lead leg. As with many single-leg defenses, I begin by moving his head to the outside of my body. However, instead of focusing on freeing my leg from his grasp, I immediately drop down to my rear knee and dive forward to attack his rear leg with a toehold. Once I've got the hold locked in, I roll over to my back, sweep my opponent to his back using my legs, and crank on the submission. It's a crafty technique because rarely will your opponent see it coming.

My opponent has shot in for a single-leg takedown with his head positioned to the inside of my body. To increase my defensive options, I immediately place my right hand on the right side of his head and begin moving it toward the outside of my body.

I move my opponent's head to the outside of my body.

I drop down to my left knee and grab the top of my opponent's right foot using my left hand.

I hook my right arm around the outside of my opponent's right leg.

Dropping down to my left elbow, I wrap my right arm around the outside of my opponent's right leg and then grab my left wrist with my right hand. At the same time, I move my right leg between my opponent's legs and then hook it around the back of his right leg.

Keeping my grip locked tight, I roll over onto my left shoulder and kick my right leg into the back of my opponent's left leg.

As I roll toward my back, I keep my grip locked tight and my right leg hooked over the top of my opponent's left leg.

Using my grips, I move my opponent's trapped right leg over to the right side of my head.

Rolling toward my right shoulder, I elevate my left leg and begin hooking it over my right foot.

I hook the crook of my left leg over my right foot, trapping my opponent's free leg and preventing him from scrambling. To apply the ankle lock, I drive the toes of his right foot in a clockwise direction using my left hand. At the same time, I drive his right ankle in a clockwise direction by pulling my right arm toward me. The combination of these actions puts a tremendous amount of pressure on the joints in his leg, forcing him to tap.

Dave Camarillo

Flying Triangle from Outside Single-Leg Defense

In this sequence I demonstrate how to defend against the single-leg takedown by utilizing a flying triangle. When playing guard, the most difficult part about locking in the triangle is maneuvering your leg over your opponent's arm to assume the triangle position. This isn't a problem in this scenario because both of your opponent's arms are wrapped around your lead leg, making it very easy to throw your leg over his shoulder and trap his head between your thighs. All you have to do is establish head and arm control to support your body weight, leap into the air, and move your free leg into position. The technique itself isn't that complicated—the most difficult part is getting over your fear of jumping into your opponent with one of your legs trapped. However, this can be remedied with practice. In my opinion, there are only two downsides to utilizing this technique in competition. First, it can sometimes be difficult to establish solid grips on your opponent's body, especially if it's late in the fight and he's covered in sweat. Second, if you for some reason fail with the technique, you will be on your back with your opponent on top of you. But once again, the more you practice this technique in training, the less likely you will be to fail with it.

Jared has shot in and secured control of my right leg.

As Jared lifts my right leg toward his chest to secure the single-leg position, I move my right shin to the outside of his body, place my left hand on the top of his head, and grab his left triceps with my right hand. Establishing both grips is very important because they support your weight as you execute the flying attack.

I secure a collar tie by hooking my left hand around the back of Jared's head. Next, I support my weight using my grips, leap off my left foot, and throw my leg over his right shoulder.

4

Having to support all of my weight, Jared has no choice but to lower me to the mat, putting him in my guard. Notice how I still have both of my grips.

5

I release my collar tie, grab Jared's left arm using my left hand, and then move his arm toward the left side of my body. It is important to notice that I have arched my hips to make it easier to slide his arm across my torso.

6

I drop my hips, trapping Jared's left arm on the left side of my body. To set up the triangle submission, I grab my left instep using my right hand.

7

I pull my left leg toward my body, which forces Jared's head to drop into my abdomen. Next, I hook the crook of my right leg over my left foot.

8

I curl my right leg downward, which forces my left leg into the back of Jared's head. To lock the triangle choke tight, I wrap my right arm around the left side of Jared's head and over my left knee. Next, I wrap my left arm around the outside of my left knee. To get the submission, I curl my legs down, pinch my knees together, and use my hands to pull my left knee toward my chest.

Part Three
The Clinch

THE DIRTY BOXING CLINCH
(p. 204-209)

World-class wrestlers like Randy Couture and Jon Fitch have demonstrated the effectiveness of the dirty boxing clinch, making it a mandatory position for all MMA fighters to learn. Establishing the dirty boxing clinch is rather simple—all it entails is securing a single collar tie by wrapping one hand around the back of your opponent's head. On the surface, it doesn't seem like a very dominant hold because your opponent still has both of his hands to strike with, but the goal is to use your collar tie to constantly disrupt your opponent's balance and base. As he struggles to regain his balance, you pummel his face and body with punches and knee strikes. The key to success with this position is to never let your opponent reacquire his base. If you allow him to regain his balance, he gains the ability to counter your hold and land punches to your face. In this section, you will learn several ways to keep your opponent's balance and base shattered, as well as how to use his lack of balance to land strikes and execute a throw. In addition to offense, this section also demonstrates how to defend against the dirty boxing clinch by preventing your opponent from establishing a solid collar tie.

THE MUAY THAI CLINCH
(p. 210-221)

The Muay Thai clinch is very similar to the dirty boxing clinch, except instead of wrapping just one hand around the back of your opponent's head, you wrap both of your hands around the back of his head. In addition to allowing you to disrupt your opponent's base by dragging his head from side to side, you gain the ability

to disrupt his base by pulling his head downward. However, with both of your hands tied up with your control, you lose the ability to punch your opponent in the face. As a result, your primary strikes from the Muay Thai clinch are knee strikes to the body. In addition to demonstrating how to batter your opponent's body with straight and side knees, this section also demonstrates how to use the Muay Thai clinch to shatter your opponent's base and execute a highly effective throw. In conclusion, this section offers three methods for escaping the Muay Thai clinch. One allows you to return to a neutral tie-up position, and the other two break your opponent's grip on your head and create an opening to land strikes. Deciding which technique to use in a fight is a matter of preference, but I recommend learning all of them because some techniques work better on certain opponents. If one doesn't work, you immediately switch to another. When it comes to being trapped in the Muay Thai clinch, you never want to be short on escapes.

OVER-UNDER CLINCH / HEAD AND ARM CLINCH
(p. 222-224)

The over-under clinch and head-and-arm clinch are considered neutral positions because both you and your opponent have the same arm positioning. For example, with the over-under clinch, you have one overhook and one underhook, and your opponent has one overhook and one underhook. With neither one of you having a dominant hold, you both have the exact same options at your disposal. In this section, you will learn how to get the upper hand in these neutral tie-up positions by obtaining a body lock

THE ULTIMATE MIXED MARTIAL ARTIST

201

and off-balancing your opponent, which in turn allows you to execute takedowns and strikes.

DOUBLE UNDERHOOK CLINCH
(p. 226-229)

In this section you will learn how to transition to a double underhook bodylock from a neutral clinch position and then execute an inside trip, which is not only a low-risk maneuver, but also one of the most effective takedowns that you can execute from the double underhook position. In addition to this, you will also learn two countering techniques for when your opponent manages to establish the double underhook clinch. The first is a simple escape, and the second is a highly effective throw that allows you to put your opponent on his back.

BACK CONTROL CLINCH
(p. 231-239)

This section opens with three techniques for establishing the back-control clinch. The first two demonstrate how to transition from neutral tie-up positions to your opponent's back, and the last demonstrates how to establish back control when your opponent throws strikes from the outside. Next, the section covers four highly effective takedowns, all of which involve lifting your opponent off the mat and dumping him to his back. They key to success with each of these techniques is initiating your attack the instant you secure the back-control clinch. With it being a very dominant hold, a lot of fighters feel safe when they reach the position and take a moment to breathe, but this allows their opponents to begin establishing their base and begin countering. To increase your odds at executing an effective takedown, you want to off-balance your opponent the instant you take his back and then lift him into the air using one of the techniques demonstrated in this section. As you will see, it is also very important to shift your opponent's body horizontally once he is off the mat. If you fail to do this, your opponent will often be able to post his feet on the mat as you drop him, thwarting your takedown attempt. When you turn him sideways once his feet are in the air, his ability to counter drops significantly. In conclusion, this section offers a highly effective throw that you can execute when your opponent secures back control.

OPPONENT PRESSED AGAINST THE CAGE
(p. 241-252)

In this section you will learn how to turn the cage into a strategic weapon by pinning your opponent up against the fence and brutalizing him with an assortment of attacks, including shoulder slams, elbow strikes, and double and single-leg takedowns. You will also learn how to counter your opponent's most common submission attempt when in this position—the standing guillotine. It is strongly suggested that you spend an ample amount of time practicing the techniques in this section because the cage can be a formidable weapon when utilized correctly. It's not necessary to base your entire game on cage tactics as some fighters do, but it can be extremely beneficial to have at least a few tricks up your sleeve.

OPPONENT PRESSING YOU AGAINST THE CAGE
(p. 254-266)

As mentioned in the previous introduction, there are many fighters who base a large part of their game on cage tactics. Their sole mission is to drive you back into the fence, trap you there, and then punish you with attacks. Just as you must learn how to avoid submissions and defend against your opponent's strikes, you must also learn how to escape when your back is on the cage. It doesn't matter if your footwork is exceptional—eventually you will find yourself in this compromising position. In this section, you will learn a number of highly effective countering options. You will learn how to reverse your opponent and pin his back against the cage, execute an assortment of takedowns, and even lock in submissions. While training to pin your opponent up against the cage can be a lot more fun, this is one section you don't want to overlook.

Jon Fitch

Punching from Dirty Boxing Clinch

In this sequence I demonstrate how to strike your way into the dirty boxing clinch and then punish your opponent with uppercuts and hooks. Although the dirty boxing clinch might not look like a dominating hold because you have one hand tied up on your opponent's head and he has both of his hands free, it can be a devastating position when utilized correctly. The goal is to keep your opponent off balance, which can be accomplished by using your collar tie to force his head downward and to one side or the other, making it difficult for him to defend against your strikes or land strikes of his own. The instant your opponent reestablishes his balance, you change your angle and dive his head in a different direction, forcing him to step and once again reestablish his base. Remember, where the head goes the body follows. However, it is important mention that you will most likely not be able to maintain the dirty boxing clinch for a prolonged period of time. If your opponent begins to escape your hold, you want to use your dominant positioning to either create separation, tie him up in a more dominant clinch, or execute the throw shown later in this section.

Dave and I are in orthodox stances, searching for an opening to attack.

Rotating my hips in a counterclockwise direction, I come up onto the ball of my right foot and throw a cross at Dave's face.

I step my left foot forward, rotate my hips in a clockwise direction, and establish the dirty boxing clinch by wrapping my left hand around the back of Dave's head. Notice how I position my left forearm in front of his right shoulder. This prevents him from driving his body into me.

Pulling Dave's head down and toward my right side, I throw a right uppercut to his jaw.

As Dave steps his right foot forward to reestablish his base and balance, I slide my right leg in a counterclockwise direction across the mat. From this new position, I can once again disrupt his balance and land strikes.

Pushing Dave's head downward, I throw a right hook to the side of his face.

Randy Couture

Striking from the Dirty Boxing Clinch

When you establish the dirty boxing clinch and begin landing punches to your opponent's head, his primary objective will be to regain his balance and square his hips with your hips. If he eliminates your dominant angle in this fashion, he can defend against your strikes and begin landing strikes of his own. To prevent him from leveling the playing field, a good tactic is to switch your collar tie from one side to the other the instant he turns into you. This allows you to once again disrupt his balance using your collar tie, which in turn allows you to continue to land strikes to his face. The instant he finds his balance again and squares his hips with your body, you switch back to your initial collar tie. This is a critical technique to learn because a lot of fighters will quickly reacquire their balance. If you don't quickly change your angle, there is a good chance you will eat some powerful punches.

I've established the dirty boxing clinch on Ryan by securing a left collar tie and driving his head downward.

With Ryan off balance, I throw a right uppercut to his face.

I pull my right arm back and angle my elbow outward.

I deliver a right elbow to the top of Ryan's head.

To keep Ryan off balance, I need to switch my collar ties. To accomplish this, I press my right forearm into the left side of his neck. At the same time, I take an outward step with my right foot.

I secure a right collar tie by wrapping my right hand around the back of Ryan's head. Once accomplished, I release my left collar tie and slide my left foot across the mat in a counterclockwise direction.

Keeping Ryan off balance by pulling his head down using my right collar tie, I land a left uppercut to his jaw.

Dirty Boxing Clinch to Hip Throw

As I mentioned earlier, it can be difficult to maintain the dirty boxing for a prolonged period of time. If you feel your opponent is recovering his balance and he is about to strip you of your control, it can be a wise move to use your dominant position to transition into another clinch. In this sequence, I demonstrate how to use the dirty boxing clinch to establish a dominant underhook. Once accomplished, you can execute a powerful hip throw by stepping into your opponent, rotating so that your back is pressed up against his chest, dropping your hips beneath your opponent's hips, and then using an upward bump along with your underhook to cast him over your body and to his back. If you look at the photos below, you'll notice that as my opponent falls to the mat, I drop down with him and maintain my grips on his body. This hinders him from scrambling and allows me to secure the side control position.

I've established the dirty boxing clinch on Dave by hooking my left hand around the back of his head.

To transition from the dirty boxing clinch to underhook control, I dive my right arm underneath his left arm.

I slide my right arm underneath Dave's left arm and then wrap my right hand over his left shoulder to secure my hold.

4

I step my left foot between Dave's legs and then drive my head into the left side of his head, forcing him to lean toward his right.

5

Rotating my body in a counterclockwise direction, I step my right foot in front of Dave's body, drop my hips below his hips, drive into his left side using my right underhook, and clasp my hands together behind his back. Notice how my actions begin lifting him off his feet.

6

Continuing to rotate my body in a counterclockwise direction, I throw Dave over my hips.

7

As Dave lands on his back, I drop down with him. Notice how I have maintained my grips to prevent him from scrambling.

Knee from Dirty Boxing Clinch

In this sequence I establish the dirty boxing clinch, but before I can unleash punches to my opponent's face using my free hand, he regains his balance and attempts to break my control using his hands. To prevent him from accomplishing his goal, I grab his far wrist with my free hand and pull it into me. Although this ties up both of my hands and makes it impossible for me to punch, I now have my opponent moving toward my body, which allows me to land a powerful knee to his midsection.

I've secured the dirty boxing clinch on Dave by wrapping my left hand around the back of his neck and pulling his head down.

Keeping Dave's head down using my left hand, I grab his left wrist with my right hand.

I lean my weight forward, causing Dave to counter my action by leaning his weight forward.

With Dave's weight moving forward, I pull his left arm into me using my right hand and deliver a right knee strike to his abdomen.

Keeping Dave's left arm elevated, I pull my right leg back into my stance and then throw a lead knee into his vulnerable midsection.

I return to the dirty boxing clinch. From here, I will continue to disrupt Dave's balance and strike.

Jon Fitch

Defending against the Dirty Boxing Clinch

In this sequence my opponent throws his right hand forward, but instead of trying to land a cross to my face, he wraps his hand around the back of my head in an attempt to secure the dirty boxing clinch. Before he can close the distance and drive his forearm into my chest, which would give him the leverage he needs to disrupt my balance, I circle my lead forearm into the crook of his outstretched arm and plant my hand on his shoulder. To create distance between us, I simply drive his body away from me. Once accomplished, I have the room I need to throw a cross at his exposed chin. Remember, you always want to make your opponent pay for his attacks to shatter his confidence and make him more hesitant about being offensive.

1 Dave has secured a right collar tie. I need to execute a counter before he can pull my head down and begin landing strikes.

2 I slide my left forearm down the inside of Dave's right arm.

3 I place my left hand on the inside of Dave's right shoulder and then shatter his collar tie by pushing his body away from mine.

4 Having created distance between our bodies, I immediately follow up with a right cross.

Erin Toughill

Muay Thai Clinch Positioning

In this sequence I demonstrate how to position your arms to lock in a proper Muay Thai clinch. The goal is not only to obtain control of your opponent's head, but also to hinder his body movement to prevent him from countering your dominant hold. There are three steps to accomplishing both aspects. First, position your forearms vertically against his collar bones. This prevents him from driving into you and either shooting for a takedown or establishing a body lock. Next, wrap one hand around the base of his skull, and then place your opposite hand on top of your first hand. This provides you with the leverage needed to pull his head downward and disrupt his base. Lastly, pinch your elbows together to limit his side-to-side head movement and further disrupt his balance. Once accomplished, you will be in the perfect position to utilize the attacks demonstrated in this section.

1

Neil and I are in close range, looking for an opening to attack.

2

To establish the Muay Thai clinch, I begin by placing my left elbow in front of Neil's right shoulder and pressing my left forearm into the right side of his neck.

3

I wrap my left hand around the back of Neil's head, press my right forearm in front of his left shoulder, and then wrap my right hand over my left hand. To disrupt Neil's balance and base, I use my grips to pull his head down. With my arms positioned in front of his shoulders, he is unable to drive his body into me.

Evading Strikes to Muay Thai Clinch

In this sequence I demonstrate how to establish the Muay Thai clinch when your opponent throws a rear hook. The first step is to block your opponent's strike, which can be accomplished by performing an outside block using your lead arm. Instead of pulling your arm back into your stance once you've executed the block, you slide your forearm down your opponent's extended arm, position your forearm vertically against his collar bone to prevent him from shooting forward, and wrap your hand around the back of his skull. This gives you the dirty boxing clinch. To transition into the Muay Thai clinch, immediately shoot your rear hand forward, position your forearm against his collar bone, and then wrap your rear hand over your lead hand. Once accomplished, the final step is to use your control to pull your opponent's head down to disrupt his balance and create openings for strikes.

1 Neil and I are in close range, looking for an opening to attack.

2 Neil throws an overhand right. To defend against his punch and set up the Muay Thai clinch, I shoot my left arm forward into the crook of his arm, stifling his strike.

3 As Neil's punch is absorbed by my left arm, I wrap my left hand around the base of his skull and secure my first collar tie.

4 I shoot my right arm forward, position my right elbow in front of Neil's left shoulder, and wrap my right hand over my left hand.

5 I secure the Muay Thai clinch by wrapping my right hand over my left hand. To disrupt Neil's base and balance, I use my grips to pull his head downward.

Shawn Yarborough

Rear Knee from Muay Thai Clinch

Below I demonstrate how to deliver a straight rear knee to your opponent's midsection from the Muay Thai clinch. If you look at the first photo in the sequence, you'll notice that instead of keeping my body erect, I sprawl my hips back, drop my elevation, and shatter his base and balance by pulling his head toward the mat using my grips. The combination of these actions creates separation between our bodies and permits me to throw a very powerful knee strike to his abdomen. Where a lot of people go wrong with this technique is they attempt to drive their knee upward into their opponent's body, which causes their knee to skim across their opponent's torso. Although it's still possible to land the knee in this fashion, it doesn't produce the same devastating effects as when you maximize the potential energy of your strike by driving your knee straight into your target. For the best results, you want to aim for the solar plexus.

Using my grips, I pull Lance's head down, move my hips away from his hips, and come up onto the ball of my right foot.

Keeping Lance's head down, I drive my right knee forward.

Coming up onto the ball of my left foot, I drive my right knee horizontally into Lance's sternum.

Anuwat Kaewsamrit

Lead Knee from Muay Thai Clinch

In this sequence I demonstrate how to throw a lead knee from the Muay Thai clinch. While it is possible to simply elevate your lead leg off the mat and drive your knee into your opponent's body, you can generate much more power in your strike by first switching your stance. If you look at the photos below, you'll notice that I accomplish this by stepping my lead foot behind me. However, I don't step linearly. Instead, I pivot on the rear foot and circle my lead leg in a counterclockwise direction across the canvas. With my arms still controlling my opponent's head, this twists his body, which disrupts his balance and exposes the right side of his torso. To capitalize on that opening, I drive my left leg forward and land a powerful knee to his liver.

1) I've established the Muay Thai clinch on my opponent.

2) To disrupt my opponent's base and balance, I step my left leg behind me. Notice how this twists his body in a counterclockwise direction and exposes his midsection.

3) Keeping my opponent off balance using my grips, I drive my left knee into his abdomen.

Side Knee from Muay Thai Clinch

Although the side knee isn't nearly as devastating as the straight knee, it is a valuable weapon to have in the clinch because it's a very quick strike that is hard to defend against. Instead of dropping your hips back as you would when executing a rear straight knee, keep your posture erect and lift your rear leg off the mat. Just as you would when performing an outside check, you want to angle your knee toward the outside of your body at a forty-five-degree angle. Once you've elevated your knee up past your opponent's waist, you sweep your leg horizontally and strike his ribs using the inside portion of your knee. As I mentioned, the strike most likely won't cause serious damage, but several of them can wear your opponent down over time and rack up points on the judges' scorecards.

1 I've established the Muay Thai clinch on Neil.

2 I elevate my right foot off the mat. Notice how I've pointed my knee toward the outside of my body at a forty-five-degree angle.

3 Having elevated my right knee to waist level, I sweep it horizontally into Neil's ribs, striking with the inside portion of my knee.

Shawn Yarborough

Off-Balance Opponent to Knee Strike

In this sequence I demonstrate how to disrupt your opponent's balance from the Muay Thai clinch using a foot sweep, which creates an opportunity to throw a knee strike to his face. However, the sweep can be a little tricky. To pull it off effectively, you want to sweep your lead foot into your opponent's lead leg. At the same time, you must force his head in the opposite direction using your arms. When first starting out, it can be difficult to move your upper body and lower body in opposite directions, but after some practice, you will find that it is not as hard as you first thought. When preformed properly, your opponent's lead leg gets pushed in one direction and his head in another, shattering his base. Before he can reestablish his balance, you deliver a devastating knee strike to his jaw.

I have secured the Muay Thai clinch on Lance.

To shatter Lance's base and balance, I force his head in a counterclockwise direction using my grips. At the same time, I sweep my left foot across the mat toward his left foot. It is important to note that my upper body is moving in a counterclockwise direction while my lower body is moving in a clockwise direction. This can often be difficult when first starting out, so it demands a lot of practice.

Still forcing Lance in a counterclockwise direction using my grips, I strike his instep using my left foot.

4

I chop Lance's left foot toward the outside of his body using my left foot, totally destroying his balance. Notice how I have kept his head tilted toward his right side using my grips.

5

Before Lance can reestablish his balance, I place my left foot on the mat and skip my right foot behind me.

6

Keeping Lance's head down, I throw my right knee toward his face.

7

I land a straight right knee to Lance's face. It is important to note that when striking the body with the straight knee, you want to send your knee horizontally into your target. However, the straight knee to the face has more of a vertical trajectory.

Shawn Yarborough

Throw from Muay Thai Clinch

Tripping your opponent is illegal in Muay Thai competition. A trip is defined as putting any part of your body behind your opponent's body and then forcing him to fall over it. As a result, Muay Thai practitioners have devised several effective takedowns that do not fall into the trip category, including the technique demonstrated below. From the Muay Thai clinch, you step your rear foot forward and to the outside of your opponent's lead foot, and then force his body over your leg using your arms. Unable to take an outward step to maintain his balance, he has no choice but to fall to the mat. It's considered a legal technique because you step off to your opponent's side rather than behind his body. While there are no rules prohibiting you from tripping your opponent in MMA, this is still a good technique to learn because it will often catch your opponent off guard. When you secure the Muay Thai clinch, he will most likely be focused on defending your knee strikes to his body instead of takedowns, allowing you to quickly throw him to the mat.

1

I have established the Muay Thai clinch on Lance.

2

Keeping Lance's head down using my grips, I step my right foot forward and to the outside of his left leg.

3

Without moving my right foot, I force Lance in a clockwise direction using my grips. Unable to take an outward step with his left leg to maintain his balance, he begins falling toward the mat.

4

Continuing to turn Lance in a clockwise direction using my grips, he trips over my right leg and falls to the mat.

Counter Opponent's Muay Thai Clinch Counter

As you have learned, when you establish the Muay Thai clinch and pull your opponent's head down, there are all sorts of nasty strikes that you can deliver. To hinder your attacks, your opponent's primary method of defense will be to straighten his posture and arch his head backward in an attempt to break your grips. As long as you have established proper grips, the majority of the time you will be able to overpower him and force his head down. However, occasionally you'll go up against a fighter who has a tremendous amount of strength in his neck. In such a scenario, instead of wasting energy with this battle, utilizing the technique demonstrated in the sequence below is an excellent option. To pull it off, simply release one of your collar ties. With one less hand holding his head down, it will usually fling backward. Before he can bring his head back forward, place your free hand on his chin and then drive his body backward. This shatters his balance, causes his posture to become even more erect, and makes his entire midsection vulnerable to strikes. To capitalize on that vulnerability, deliver a straight knee to his midsection.

1 I have secured the Muay Thai clinch on Neil, but he prevents me from pulling his head down by standing erect and pulling his head back.

2 Instead of trying to overpower Neil, I release my collar ties. As his head flings backward due to his defense, I position my right palm in from of his chin.

3 Before Neil can drop his head, I place my right palm on his chin and force it backward, disrupting his balance.

4 Keeping Neil off balance using my right palm, I throw a straight right knee into his exposed midsection.

MUAY THAI CLINCH

DEFENSIVE TECHNIQUES

Shawn Yarborough

Escaping Muay Thai Clinch (option 1)

When your opponent establishes the Muay Thai clinch, it's in your best interest to escape as quickly as possible. There are many ways to do this, but the technique demonstrated in the sequence below is one of my favorites because not only does it allow you to escape the Muay Thai clinch, but it also allows you to establish a Muay Thai clinch of your own. To begin, wrap an arm over your opponent's arm and then drive your hand into the side of his jaw. This cranks his head to the side and creates separation between your bodies. While keeping him at bay in this fashion, dig your opposite hand up between his arms, establish a collar tie, and drive your forearm into his collarbone to prevent him from driving into you. Once accomplished, you can release your cross face grip on his jaw, dig your second hand up between his arms, and secure your second collar tie, giving you the Muay Thai clinch. For the best results, you want to utilize this technique the instant your opponent cups his hands behind your head. If you are slow to react and allow him to pull your head down, he will be able to use his dominant position to off-balance you and land strikes, making it much more difficult to employ your defense.

1

Lance has secured the Muay Thai clinch. Before he can begin landing strikes, I must make my escape.

2

I place my left hand on Lance's right hip to keep his body at bay. At the same time, I slide my right arm over his left arm and place my hand on the left side of his chin.

3

I drive Lance's head away from me an in a clockwise direction using my right hand. Notice how this creates separation between our bodies.

4

Keeping Lance's head cranked to the side to maintain distance between us, I slide my left arm upward between his arms.

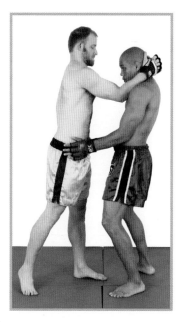

THE ULTIMATE MIXED MARTIAL ARTIST

Still forcing Lance's head away using my right hand, I reach my left hand over his right shoulder and toward the back of his head.

I cup my left palm around the back of Lance's head, securing a collar tie. Next, I remove my right palm from his chin and turn my body in a clockwise direction. Notice how this creates separation between our bodies.

Having created space between us with my clockwise rotation, I begin sliding my right arm up between Lance's arms.

I cup my right hand over my left hand, securing the Muay Thai clinch. Immediately I pull Lance's head down and begin setting up an attack.

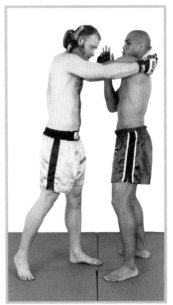

Anderson Silva

Escaping Muay Thai Clinch (option 2)

In the previous Muay Thai clinch escape, Shawn demonstrated how to cross face your opponent to create distance between your bodies, and then use that distance to pummel your arms to the inside of his arms to secure a Muay Thai clinch of your own. It's an excellent technique, but when your opponent locks in a solid hold, it can sometimes be difficult to create the needed separation. In such a scenario, the technique shown below is an excellent option. Instead of trying to drive your opponent away, you shatter his hold by driving one of his arms downward and the other arm up and over your head. It's doesn't land you in a dominant clinch like the previous technique, but it allows you to escape a very compromising position. It also sets you up perfectly to land a knee strike to your opponent's midsection.

Feijao has secured the Muay Thai clinch. Before he can close the distance between us and pull my head down, I reach my left arm over his right arm and drive my forearm into his throat.

Keeping Feijao at bay using my left forearm, I place my right hand underneath his left elbow.

Rotating my body slightly, I drive Feijao's left arm over my head. At the same time, I trap his right arm using my left arm.

Keeping Feijao off balance using my grips, I drive my left knee upward into his ribcage.

Escaping Muay Thai Clinch (option 3)

In this sequence I demonstrate a very quick yet powerful escape from the Muay Thai clinch. If you look at the photos below, you'll notice that my actions are rather simple—all I do is rotate my body in a counterclockwise direction and throw my right arm over my opponent's arms and toward the left side of my body. As my right shoulder drives into his left forearm, it puts a tremendous amount of pressure on his grips and tears his left hand from my head. However, having turned my body away from my opponent, it is possible for him to reach his arms around my torso and establish a body lock. To prevent him from accomplishing this, as well as make him pay for his attack, I rotate in a clockwise direction and throw lead back elbow into his jaw. The strike knocks my opponent to his left, allowing me to immediately follow up with a rear side elbow to the exact same spot on his jaw. The downside to this technique is that it can sometimes be difficult to shatter your opponent's grips when he has already established a dominant hold. For the best results, this technique should be employed the instant your opponent grabs your head. If you allow him to use his grips to force your head downward, it is much more difficult to pull off.

Feijao has secured the Muay Thai clinch. Before he can launch an attack, I hook my left hand over the crook of his right arm.

I reach my right arm over Feijao's head toward the right side of his body.

As I move my right arm toward the right side of Feijao's body, my right shoulder shatters his left collar tie.

Utilizing the space I created, I throw a right back elbow into the side of Feijao's jaw.

I follow through with my right elbow by rotating my hips in a clockwise direction.

As my right elbow slides off the side of Feijao's face, I continue my rotation and throw a left side elbow.

I land a left side elbow to Feijao's face.

Randy Couture

Step-Around Takedown from Over-Under Body Lock

A lot of times when you establish the over-under clinch, you are able to clasp your hands together behind your opponent's back. You don't have as dominant of a body lock as you do when you secure double underhooks, but there are still several ways to take your opponent to the mat, with the technique demonstrated below being one of the highest percentage ones. Instead of lifting his feet off the mat and chucking him through the air, you simply step behind your opponent and force him to trip over your leg. It is important to mention that this technique is most frequently utilized from a double underhook body lock, but because both of your arms are underneath your opponent's arms, he can post a hand on the mat as you take him down and possibly work up to his knees or escape. The nice part about utilizing the step-around from the over-under clinch is that you have an overhook on his near arm, which makes it impossible for him to post his hand on the mat. This allows you to immediately drop down into side control.

From the over-under clinch, I have managed to lock my hands together behind Ryan's back using an S-grip.

Rotating my hips in a clockwise direction, I step my left leg behind Ryan's right leg.

I step my right foot behind my left and drive my weight forward. With my legs preventing Ryan from stepping backward, he loses his balance.

I rotate my body in a counterclockwise direction and drive Ryan toward the mat. Notice how I have kept my hands locked tightly together.

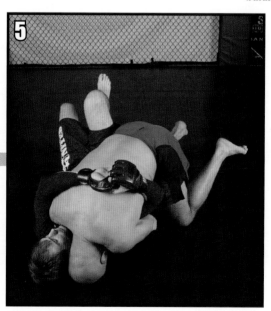

Having stepped around Ryan's legs, I land on top of him in side control and can immediately begin a ground attack.

Anuwat Kaewsamrit

Off-Balance to Knee Strike from Head-and-Arm

A lot of opponents are masters at defending against your strikes when you establish the Muay Thai clinch. If you're up against such an opponent, this is a good technique to employ because it forces him to bend forward at the waist and drop the elevation of his head, creating the perfect opportunity to land a knee strike to his face. To set it up, you must first establish the proper grips. This can be accomplished by releasing your rear collar tie and sliding your hand down to your opponent's biceps, a grip that is commonly referred to as a biceps tie. The biceps tie is critical because it allows you to position your elbow underneath your opponent's elbow, giving you the leverage you need to lift his arm upward. To shatter his balance and destroy his defenses, you circle around his body, pull down on his head with your remaining collar tie, and lift his arm upward using your biceps tie. As your opponent's body is thrust awkwardly forward, you throw a knee strike to his face. The key to success with this technique is being fluid with your movements. The instant you off-balance your opponent, immediately transition into the knee strike. If you delay, he will be able to recover his balance, straighten his body, and avoid your attack.

1 I have established head and arm control by securing a left collar tie, positioning my right arm to the inside of my opponent's left arm, and grabbing his left bicep using my right hand.

2 I step my right foot forward and to the outside of my opponent's lead leg. At the same time, I pull his head in a counterclockwise direction using my left collar tie and lift his left arm upward using my right hand.

3 Continuing to pull my opponent's head in a counterclockwise direction and lift up on his left arm, I slide my left foot across the mat in a counterclockwise direction. Notice how my actions shatter his base.

4 Before my opponent can reestablish his balance and base, I drive my left knee upward into his face.

Karo Parisyan

Outside Trip from Head-and-Arm Clinch

In this sequence I demonstrate how to execute an outside trip when you establish a collar tie with one hand and a triceps grip with the other. When your opponent's legs are somewhat close to your legs, executing the move is as simple as stepping forward, hooking your opponent's leg with your leg, and then sweeping his leg out from underneath him while driving his upper body toward the mat using your grips. If your opponent's legs are farther away, you'll probably need to hop forward once you've hooked his leg in order to close the distance and gain the leverage needed to execute the throw. The nice part about this technique is the simplicity of the grips involved. A lot of throws require you to establish elaborate grips, which can be difficult to maintain when your opponent is covered in sweat. You don't have that issue with this technique.

I have established head and arm control by securing a right collar tie and gripping slightly above Neil's right elbow using my left hand.

I step my left foot to the outside of Neil's right leg. If you do not step far enough to the side, you won't have the room needed to bring your right leg forward to execute the outside trip.

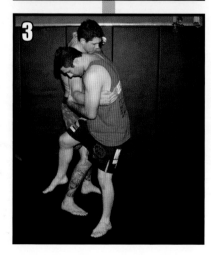

Still controlling Neil's right arm using my left hand, I use my collar tie to push his upper body to his right side, forcing the majority of his weight onto his right leg. At the same time, I swing my right leg around the outside of his right leg.

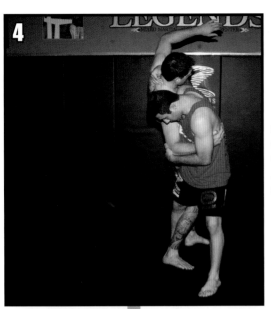

Continuing to push Neil's upper body toward his right side using my collar tie, I circle my right leg all the way around his right leg and then plant my foot between his legs.

Driving forward and twisting in a counterclockwise direction, I force Neil over my planted right leg and send him flying through the air.

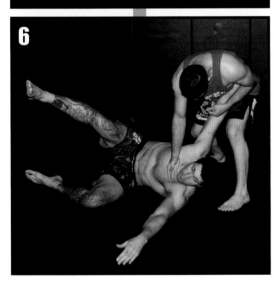

Having reduced my forward momentum the instant Neil's body went airborne, I remain standing as he crashes down on his back. It is important to notice that I still have control of his right arm. From here, I can work to secure an armbar, drop down on top of him and secure side control, or remain standing and punish him with strikes.

Pummeling

The over-under clinch is a neutral position because both you and your opponent have one overhook and one underhook. Although there are many techniques that you can execute from the over-under clinch, your opponent has those same options. To get the upper hand, it is often in your best interest to transition to a more dominant clinch, such as double underhooks. In this sequence, I demonstrate how to do that by pummeling. The goal is to swim your overhook arm underneath your opponent's underhook arm, which in turn allows you to clasp your hands together behind his back. However, as you work to eliminate your opponent's underhook, he will most likely do the same to you on the opposite side. For example, as you swim your right overhook underneath your opponent's underhook, he swims his right overhook underneath your left underhook. When both of you are successful, you end up back in the over-under clinch, just on opposite sides. This can often be a back-and-forth battle, but the more you practice pummeling, the better you will get at eliminating your opponent's underhook while preventing him from doing the same to you. Therefore, I recommend training the drill below as often as possible.

Dave and I are in the over-under clinch, both trying to get the upper hand.

In an attempt to establish double underhooks, I pummel my left arm underneath Dave's right arm. However, as I do this, he begins pummeling his left arm underneath my right arm.

I slide my left arm underneath Dave's right armpit, establishing an underhook. Not wanting me to get the upper hand, he slides his left arm underneath my right arm.

As I establish a deep left underhook, Dave establishes a deep left underhook. We are back to the original position, only now our overhook and underhook are reversed. We will keep going like this until one of us establishes double underhooks.

Jon Fitch

Inside Trip from Double Underhook Control

This technique comes into play when you manage to pummel both of your arms underneath your opponent's arms and establish a double underhook body lock. To set up the inside trip from this dominant hold, all you have to do is hook your rear leg around the inside of your opponent's lead leg to trap his leg in place. Once accomplished, it's simply a matter of rotating your opponent's body toward his trapped leg. Unable to take an outward step to maintain his balance, he collapses to the mat. Personally, I like to maintain my body lock and come down on top of my opponent. Sometimes you will land in his guard, but if you are quick to react, you can often quickly jump over his legs and establish side control.

I have established a double underhook body lock by sliding my arms underneath Dave's arms and locking my hands together behind his back. For the best grip, you want to grab your left wrist with your right hand and your right wrist with your left hand.

Rotating my body in a counterclockwise direction, I hook my right leg around the inside of Dave's left leg.

As I drive my right leg backward to pull Dave's left leg out from underneath him, I turn his body toward his missing leg by rotating my upper body in a clockwise direction. Unable to step his left foot toward the outside of his body to regain his balance, he begins collapsing to the mat.

As Dave lands on his back, I begin stepping over his legs in a clockwise direction to avoid his guard and establish side control

Jon Fitch

Escaping Opponent's Double Underhooks

When your opponent secures a double underhook body lock, it's in your best interest to escape his hold as quickly as possible. With the majority of attacks in his arsenal requiring him to pull your hips into his body, the first step is to drop your level by bending at the knees and pull your hips away from him. The farther away you can position your hips, the more you weaken his grips. If you have your left foot back as I do in the photos below, the next step is to place your left forearm on his face and drive his head away from you. In addition to further weakening his hold, it also creates space between your bodies. Once you have created an opening, drive your right forearm across his neck and jaw and crank his head to the side. This allows you to create more space and pummel your left arm underneath his right arm, returning to the neutral over-under clinch.

Dave has established a double underhook body lock. I must mount my escape before he can launch an attack.

I create separation between our bodies by sliding my left foot in a counterclockwise direction across the mat. To create even more separation, I place my left forearm against the left side of Dave's head and push it away from me.

Having created separation using my left arm, I slide my right forearm across Dave's jaw line and then apply outward pressure to crank his head in a clockwise direction.

Keeping Dave's head cranked to the side, I slide my left arm to the inside of his right arm.

I slide my left arm underneath Dave's right arm, establishing a deep underhook. We are now in the neutral over-under clinch position.

Hip Throw

In this sequence I demonstrate a judo hip throw to turn the tables on your opponent when he secures a double underhook body lock. The key to being successful with this technique is stepping your lead foot between your opponent's legs and turning your body sideways the instant he clasps his hands together behind your back. This stretches his arms out and eliminates his ability to pick you up. Once accomplished, drop your hips beneath his hips, perform a back step to place your back against his chest, step in front of his rear leg, and then throw him over your hip and to the mat. It is important to mention that this technique is a lot harder to pull off when your opponent isn't wearing a gi, especially when he is covered in sweat. To increase your success, pay close attention to how to establish your grips in the sequence below. It's also important to utilize the throw when your opponent is driving his body forward, because it allows you to use his energy against him.

As Neil closes the distance between us, he drives both of his arms underneath my arms and grips his hands together in the center of my back, securing a double underhook body lock. The instant he does this, I hook both of my arms over his arms.

To prevent Neil from taking me to the mat, I need to angle my hips away from his centerline and establish a controlled lock on his upper body. I accomplish this by corkscrewing my body in a counterclockwise direction, driving his left arm upward using my right whizzer grip, and latching on to his right triceps with my left hand. If you wait too long to angle your hips away from your opponent when he secures a body lock, he will be able to gain full control of your hips, giving him a number of offensive options such as slamming you to the mat.

Maintaining my grips and continuing to corkscrew my body, I step my left foot close to my right foot and position my hips underneath Neil's hips.

4 Still corkscrewing my body in a counterclockwise direction, I sprawl my right leg around the outside of Neil's right leg. It is very important to keep a tight whizzer grip, as well as maintain a firm grip on your opponent's right arm using your left hand. If either grip is loose, your opponent will be able to pull his arm free, reestablish his base, and secure control of your back.

5 As I continue to corkscrew my body, I use my control over Neil's upper body to pull him over my right leg. With his upper body locked tight to my back and my right leg posted firmly on the mat, he has no choice but to trip over my leg and summersault toward the mat. If you look at the photos closely, you'll notice that I momentarily break my grips. The reason for this is because I don't want to injure Neil by dumping him on his head. If you're fighting, you want to keep your grips tight to control your opponent in the air and maximize the force behind the slam.

6

Before Neil can recover from the throw, I wrap my right arm around his head and simultaneously slide my right leg underneath my left leg and move my left leg over my right leg. This gives me what is known as the scarf-hold position and will allow me to begin my ground attack.

Randy Couture

Shuck to Back

The majority of the time when you establish an underhook in the clinch, your opponent will wrap his arm over your underhook and secure a tight whizzer to hinder your offensive options. However, occasionally your opponent will get lazy with his whizzer, allowing you to shuck his overhook arm over your head by executing a movement that resembles a swimmers freestyle stroke. Once accomplished, you have a clear pathway to circle around behind your opponent and take his back. The key to success with this technique is being explosive with your movements. You want to drop your level and throw your underhook over your head, just as when throwing an overhand right. If you half-ass this movement, you will not clear your opponent's arm over your head, giving him the ability to seize control of your head.

1 I'm tied up with Ryan in the clinch. I have established an underhook with my left arm, and secured inside biceps control with my right arm.

2 To begin my transition, I lean toward my right side, pull Ryan's left arm into his body using my right hand, and throw my left underhook up and over his body. Notice how this movement is similar to a swimmers freestyle stroke.

3 Continuing to swim my left arm forward, Ryan's right arm is forced over my head, creating a pathway to his back.

4 I circle behind Ryan and begin wrapping my left arm around his body. Notice how I'm still controlling his left arm with my right hand; this will allow me to wedge my left arm underneath his left arm and lock my hands together.

5 I slide my left arm underneath Ryan's left arm and then clasp my hands together, securing back control.

Head-and-Arm Clinch to Back Control

In this sequence I demonstrate how to transition from head and arm control to back control to increase your offensive options. The most important part of this technique is establishing inside control on your opponent's arm. If you look at the photos below, you'll notice that I have a right collar tie and my opponent has a left collar tie. However, I have positioned my left arm to the inside of my opponent's right arm and secured a biceps tie. Assuming this inside position allows me to elevate my opponent's arm up and over my head, which in turn allows me to spin around to his back. If you fail to secure inside control, you won't be able to move your opponent's arm out of the way. And if you fail to move his arm out of the way, he can easily prevent you from moving behind him.

Dave and I are tied up in the clinch. I've secured a collar tie with my right hand and established inside biceps control with my left hand.

Pulling Dave's head in a clockwise direction using my right collar tie, I elevate my left elbow upward. Due to my inside positioning, this lifts Dave's right arm and creates a pathway to his back.

BACK CONTROL CLINCH

OFFENSIVE TECHNIQUES

THE ULTIMATE MIXED MARTIAL ARTIST

Still pulling Dave's head in a clockwise direction using my right collar tie, I step my left foot forward and to the outside of his right leg. At the same time, I move my left arm over my head, which in turn moves Dave's right arm over my head.

Having cleared Dave's right arm, I immediately elevate my head and drive it into his right shoulder. This hinders him from moving his arm back over my head or locking in a choke.

Still pulling Dave in a clockwise direction using my collar tie, I circle around to his back and position my left arm to the inside of his left thigh. From here, I can immediately begin an attack from back control.

Jon Fitch

Armdrag to Back

In this sequence I demonstrate another method for transitioning to your opponent's back while standing. If you look at the photos below, you'll notice that the action begins when my opponent reaches his rear hand forward to secure a collar tie. Instead of letting him wrap his hand around the back of my neck and establish the dirty boxing clinch, I drive my lead forearm into the crook of his extending arm to block his attack. With our bodies close together, I quickly grab his opposite arm with my free hand. Next, I double up on that arm by grabbing it with both of my hands, securing the arm-drag position. To make the transition to his back, all I have to do is pull his arm across my body using both of my grips and circle around behind him. The key to success with this technique is speed. If you delay in the arm-drag position, there is a good chance your opponent will either break your control or use his free hand to start throwing punches to your unprotected face.

Dave and I are in orthodox stances, searching for an opening to attack.

Dave reaches his right arm forward to establish a collar tie. To prevent him from accomplishing his goal, I shoot my left hand to the inside of his right shoulder, causing my left forearm to block his arm. At the same time, I shoot my right arm forward and grab the outside of his left wrist.

I force Dave's left arm downward using my right hand. Next, I remove my left hand from his shoulder and grab his left triceps. This gives me two-on-one control. However, with Dave having a free arm to punch me with, I have to make my transition to his back quickly to avoid taking damage.

I release my right grip on Dave's left wrist and then pull his arm toward my left side using my left hand. Notice how this disrupts his balance. At the same time, I step my left foot between his legs and wrap my right arm around his back and grab his right hip.

Having removed Dave's left arm from my path, I circle around to his back and clasp my hands together, establishing back control.

Jon Fitch

Knee Bump

In MMA, the takedown shown below is very common from back control. The first step is to lift your opponent off the mat, which requires you to get your hips below his hips. While it is sometimes possible to muscle your opponent to the mat once he is elevated, a much better option is to turn his body sideways to eliminate his ability to catch himself using his feet. This is accomplished by lifting one of your legs off the mat and bumping it into your opponent's legs. Once his body is horizontal, his chances of avoiding the takedown become very small. However, it is important to mention that when you utilize the bump, you usually commit yourself to also going to the ground. If your goal is to land on top of your opponent in a dominant position, this is a great option. If your goal is to dump your opponent to the ground and remain standing, you'd be better off utilizing one of the other options in this section.

1

I have established back control on Dave.

2

I drop my hips lower than Dave's hips and then straighten my body to lift his feet off the mat.

3

With Dave elevated off the mat, I rotate my upper body in a clockwise direction to force his upper body toward my right side. At the same time, I lift my right leg off the mat and drive it in a counterclockwise direction into his right leg. The combination of these actions turns his body sideways.

4

Having swept Dave's legs out from underneath him, I drop him to the mat. From here, I can establish the side control position.

Randy Couture

Rear Body Lock Takedown

In this sequence I demonstrate a very simple way to take your opponent down when you establish a rear body lock. The first step is to unclasp your hands from around your opponent's waist and then cup them around the front of his shoulders. In addition to pinning his back to your chest, which prevents him from leaning forward, it also provides you with the leverage needed to lift his body. Once his feet are off the mat, you bump a knee into his backside to push his lower body away from you. With his legs now positioned out in front of his upper body, you can complete the takedown by simply dropping or lowering him to the mat. As you can see in the photos below, this creates the perfect way to establish the knee-on-belly position and begin your ground and pound assault.

1

I have established back control on Ryan.

2

I release my grip from around Ryan's waist, slide my arms up his body, and wrap my hands around the front of his shoulders.

3

As I lean back, I keep Ryan's back glued to my chest using my arms. At the same time, I drive my left knee into his tailbone to force his legs out from underneath him.

4

Having forced Ryan's legs out from underneath him, I drop him toward his back.

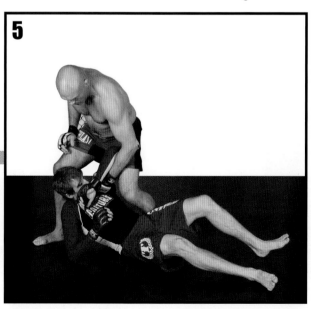

5

As Ryan lands on his back, I keep my left arm hooked around the crook of his left arm and circle around to his left side. From here, I can throw strikes from the standing position, establish the knee-on-belly position, or drop down into side control.

Jon Fitch

Throw from Back Control

This is a somewhat unorthodox takedown from back control. Instead of remaining behind your opponent, you step one leg in front of his legs. However, in order to pull this off your must alter your grips to gain better control of your opponent's head and far hip. Obtaining head control hinders him from posturing up, and obtaining control of his far hip allows you to lift him over your leg and throw him to his back. The most important attribute with this technique is speed. If you step in front of your opponent's body and hesitate, he can either elbow you in the face or sweep you to the mat by sitting back.

1

Having a difficult time taking Dave down from back control, I alter my grips by sliding my left hand down to the inside of his left leg and hooking my right arm around the left side of his neck.

2

Using my grips to elevate Dave's body, I step my left leg around to the front of his right leg.

3

Rotating my body in a clockwise direction, I hook my left hand around Dave's left hip and then use that control to pull his body up and over my left leg. At the same time, I pull down on his head using my right hand.

4

As I throw Dave over to his back, I drop down into side control.

5

To secure the side control position, I turn my left hip into Dave's left hip.

Randy Couture

Takedown off Kimura Defense

A lot of times when you secure back control your opponent will establish a kimura grip on one of your arms in an attempt to break your hands apart. While it's still possible to lift your opponent off the mat as he works to break your grips, it can be difficult to turn his body sideways to complete the takedown. The longer you delay in this position, the greater chances your opponent has of shattering your grip and applying the kimura. To avoid such dangers, the instant my opponent applies the kimura, I'll unclasp my hands, reach my free hand up between his legs, and then latch onto his wrist. Next, I'll drop my hips and lift my opponent up. With one of my arms between his legs, his body becomes very unbalanced as his feet lift off the mat, causing him to turn sideways. To complete the takedown, all I have to do is drop him to the mat. The nice part about this technique is that it gives you the option of remaining standing or dropping down on top of your opponent.

The instant I establish back control, Ryan secures a kimura grip on my right arm. He accomplishes this by grabbing my right wrist with his left hand, hooking his right arm underneath my right arm, and then grabbing his left wrist with his right hand. If I delay, he can use his grip to break my lock.

Instead of fighting Ryan's control, I release my grips, circle in a counterclockwise direction around his body, and then reach my left arm between his legs and grab his left wrist with my left hand.

Due to my altered grips, the instant I lift Ryan off the mat, his body begins falling forward.

As Ryan's head falls forward, I drop him toward the mat.

I drop Ryan to his back. From here, I have several options. I can throw strikes from the standing position, establish the knee-on-belly position, or drop down into side control.

Karo Parisyan

Osoto-Gari from Kimura Control Grip

In this sequence I demonstrate how to break your opponent's rear body lock by establishing a kimura grip and then utilize your hold to throw him to his back. The key to success is locking in your kimura grip the instant your opponent wraps his arms around your body. Although he will still be positioned behind you, it is very difficult for him to launch an effective attack with one of his arms locked up. Not having to worry about getting hefted off your feet or caught in a submission hold, you can move safely around to the side of his body, hook your near leg around his rear leg, and then execute the throw. As your opponent goes down, it is important to maintain your kimura grip. In addition to preventing your opponent from scrambling, it also allows you to make a quick transition to side control and lock in the kimura submission. Having utilized this technique in several of my fights, including those with Nick Diaz and Dave Strasser, I strongly recommend practicing it often.

Having successfully closed the distance, Neil circles behind me and locks his arms around my waist by clasping his hands together. The instant he does this, I latch on to his right wrist with my left hand and begin wrapping my right arm around the outside of his right arm.

To secure a kimura lock on Neil's right arm, I push down on his wrist with my left hand, slide my right hand underneath his right arm, and grab my left wrist with my right hand. If you have a difficult time slipping your right hand underneath your opponent's arm, which can happen when you're up against a wrestler with a strong body lock, try sucking in your belly as you drive his wrist down. Often this will create enough space to wedge your hand through and secure the kimura lock.

In order to execute osoto-gari from kimura control, I first need to break Neil's grip. I accomplish this by pressing his right wrist down into my body using my left hand, driving my right forearm upward into his right arm, and rotating my body in a clockwise direction.

Still controlling Neil's right arm with the kimura lock, I wrap my right leg around his right leg and then plant my foot to the inside of his right heel.

Maintaining the kimura lock and my right leg hook, I hop my left foot to the outside of Neil's right leg.

Now that I've positioned my body to the outside of Neil's body, I execute the osoto-gari throw by driving my upper body forward and kicking my right leg back into Neil's right leg. If you neglect to drop your head or you lose your grip, the throw will most likely not work.

As I come down with Neil, I keep my kimura lock intact. From here, I have a couple of options. I could hop my legs over to his left side and finish the kimura, or I could release my hold and establish side control on his right side.

Cage Slam to Double-Leg

In this sequence I demonstrate how to use the cage wall to help score a double-leg takedown. For the best results, I'll utilize this technique when I see that my opponent's back is about three or four feet from the fence. To set up my takedown, I'll either throw an overhand right or evade one of my opponent's strikes. In both cases, I'll immediately drop my elevation, shoot into my opponent's body, and drive him straight backward. As long as he runs into the chain link instead of one of the solid poles supporting the walls, his body will rebound back into me, allowing me to heft him off his feet and dump him to the mat. However, it should be mentioned that this technique should be reserved for when your opponent is near the cage wall. If you are both in the center of the cage, it's best to complete the double-leg using the "turning the corner" method demonstrated earlier.

1

Ryan and I are in orthodox stances, searching for an opening to attack.

2

Ryan throws a jab at my face. To evade his strike, I parry his arm toward my left side, slightly rotate my body in clockwise direction, and move my head toward my right side.

3

Before Ryan can pull his left arm back into his stance, I step my right foot forward and to the outside of his left foot, drive my left shoulder into his chest, and wrap my arms around the back of his legs.

4

I drive off my right foot, pushing Ryan toward the fence.

5

I drive Ryan forcibly into the chain link, causing his body to rebound back into me.

6

As Ryan's body rebounds off the chain link, I increase my elevation, lift his body off the mat using my arms, drive my head into his right side, and begin rotating my upper body in a counterclockwise direction.

Continuing to rotate my body and drive my head into Ryan's right side, his body turns horizontal to the mat.

As I drop Ryan to the mat, I maintain control of his legs.

To prevent Ryan from scrambling, I bend at the knees and drive my hips into his hips. At the same time I posture up to begin a ground-and-pound assault.

Shoulder Bump — *Randy Couture*

When you have an opponent pinned up against the cage, the shoulder bump is an excellent tool for distracting him and scoring points on the judges' scorecards. Although the strike looks quite harmless, it's possible to break either your opponent's nose or jaw using this technique. And even if you don't manage to break anything on your opponent's face, landing ten or twenty shoulder bumps over the course of a fight works great for wearing your opponent down. Remember, the goal in fighting is to get as nasty as possible. When you break the sport down, you'll realize that no matter what spot you end up in, there is usually some way to cause your opponent pain or discomfort.

1) I have Ryan pressed up against the fence. I have an underhook on my left side, and he has an underhook on his left side. 2) Keeping Ryan pinned against the fence by driving my right shoulder into his body, I rotate my upper body in a counterclockwise direction and pull my left shoulder away from him. 3) With a snapping motion, I rotate my upper body in a clockwise direction and drive my left shoulder into Ryan's chin.

Randy Couture

Inside Trip

When you pin your opponent up against the fence, you eliminate his ability to sprawl, which makes him susceptible to double-leg takedowns. In an attempt to hinder you from executing a double-leg, a lot of opponents will lean their back against the fence and drop their hips. Although this does in fact make it more difficult to perform a double-leg, it positions their feet out in front of their body, making them susceptible to the inside trip demonstrated below. The technique is extremely simple—all you have to do is hook your lead leg around your opponent's near calf, pull his leg out from underneath him, and then rotate his body toward his missing leg. This causes him to drop to his back, allowing you to immediately begin your ground assault.

I have Ryan pinned up against the cage. I have an underhook on my left side, and he has an underhook on his left side.

Continuing to drive into Ryan to keep him pinned against the cage, I hook my left leg around the inside of his right leg.

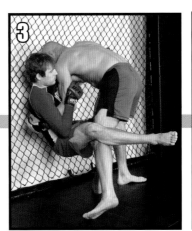

I sweep Ryan's leg out from underneath him by sliding my left foot across the mat in a counterclockwise direction. At the same time I rotate my upper body in a counterclockwise direction. The combination of these actions destroys his balance and causes him to fall toward his back.

As Ryan lands on his back, I drive my hips into his legs to prevent him from scrambling. Next, I posture up to begin my ground-and-pound assault.

Randy Couture

Cross Bump to Elbow

When I've got my opponent pinned up against the cage and we're locked up in the over-under clinch, a lot of times I will use a cross bump to create the separation I need to land an elbow strike to his face. To accomplish this, I'll place my lead leg in between my opponent's legs and then bump my knee into the inside of his far leg. At the same time, I pull his upper body in the opposite direction using my arms. The combination of these two actions disrupts his balance. As he works to reacquire that balance, I'll pull slightly away from him and deliver an elbow strike. Not wanting to lose my dominant positioning, I'll immediately drop my striking arm and pummel it underneath my opponent's arm, securing an underhook on the opposite side. Sometimes you will be able to secure a double-underhook body lock in this fashion, especially if you daze your opponent with your elbow strike, but the majority of the time he'll establish an underhook on the opposite side, returning you to the neutral over-under clinch. As I mentioned earlier, no matter what position you're in, there is usually a way to punish your opponent. The goal is acquiring techniques that allow you to dish out that punishment without sacrificing your positioning.

I have Ryan pinned against the cage. I have an underhook on my left side, and he has an underhook on his left side.

I drive my left knee against the inside of Ryan's left leg. This disrupts his balance and causes him to lean toward his right side.

Before Ryan can regain his base and balance, I pull my right shoulder away from his body and throw a right elbow strike.

I land a right elbow strike to the left side of Ryan's face.

Immediately after landing the elbow strike, I move my head to the left side of his head and dig my right arm underneath his left arm, once against establishing an underhook.

Anderson Silva

Snap-Down to Standing Guillotine

When applying submissions on the ground, the goal is to trap your opponent in a fixed position and then apply a ruthless hold. The better you pin his body, the more difficult it becomes for him to escape the submission. Finishing your opponent with a submission from the standing position is often difficult to manage because he can still move in any direction, dramatically increasing his escape routes. A perfect example is the standing guillotine. When you apply it in the center of the cage, your opponent can drop his level and attack your legs with a takedown. It's possible to hold on to the guillotine as you go down, but there is also a possibility that he will break your hold during the transition. A much better approach is to apply the standing guillotine when you have your opponent backed up against the fence, which is what I demonstrate below. To set the submission up from head and arm control, snap your opponent's head toward the floor using your collar tie. Before he can elevate his head, wrap an arm around his neck, clasp your hands together, and apply the choke. However, instead of finishing the choke by arching back, which would pull your opponent away from the fence and increase his mobility, you drive into your opponent. The harder you drive forward, the more difficult it becomes to escape the choke. However, it is important to note that applying the standing guillotine requires a great deal of energy. If you lock in the hold and your opponent doesn't quickly tap or pass out, move onto something else before burning out your arms.

I have my opponent pinned up against the cage. I'm gripping his right wrist with my left hand, and I'm using my right collar tie to pull his head toward the mat.

Keeping my opponent's right arm pinned to his side using my left hand, I release my right collar tie and slide my arm over his head.

I wrap my right biceps around the back of my opponent's neck and then dig my right forearm across his throat.

I wrap my left hand around the base of my right hand, step my right leg behind me, drop my weight onto my opponent's back, and then use both arms to drive the blade of my right wrist up into his throat.

Elbow Strike against Cage

In this sequence I demonstrate how to land elbow strikes when you pin your opponent up against the cage and secure a dominant underhook. The goal is to create enough space between you and your opponent to land effective blows, but at the same time prevent him from closing off that space by driving into you. To accomplish this, you simply wrap your underhook arm over his shoulder and then cross face him with your forearm. With his head cranked to the side, it becomes very difficult for him to move into you, allowing you to land elbows to his face. However, it is important to note that it can be difficult to hold this position for long. The majority of the time you will have an opportunity to land one or two strikes, but then you must immediately secure a dominant hold again. If you get greedy, there is a good chance your opponent will escape this compromising position.

I have my opponent pinned up against the fence. I have a deep left underhook, and I've grabbed his left wrist with my right hand.

I drive my left knee into my opponent's right thigh to disrupt his balance and pin him to the fence.

Keeping my left knee pinned to my opponent's right thigh, I hook my left arm over his right shoulder. Next, I drive my left forearm against his chin and crank his head to his left side.

With my opponent pinned against the fence, I throw a right upward elbow to his face.

Randy Couture

Knee Block Takedown

When you pin your opponent up against the cage and secure an underhook, the knee block is an excellent technique for taking him to the ground. The goal is to prevent your opponent from moving his lower body by blocking his knee with your free hand, while at the same time driving his upper body laterally using your underhook. As his upper body moves away from his legs, he collapses to the mat. However, it can be difficult to move your opponent's upper body using your underhook alone. To get him moving laterally, you must walk in the same lateral direction. This is the tricky part. With your legs positioned so close to your opponent's legs, it is easy to get both of your legs tangled up. To prevent that from happening, you want to draw an imaginary line on the mat between your bodies. As long as your feet stay on one side of the line and his on the other, you can walk past his body without hindrance. Another helpful hint is to throw your underhook arm in the direction you're heading as though you were doing a shot put. If you simply run your forearm up into his armpit, there is a good chance he will be able to hinder you from moving him laterally.

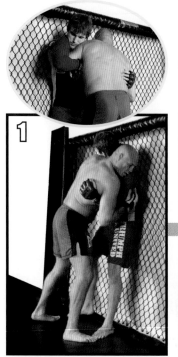

1 I have Ryan pinned against the fence. I have a left underhook, and he has a left underhook.

2 I rotate my body in a clockwise direction, bend forward at the waist, and drive my left underhook upward into Ryan's right armpit.

3 Still driving my left underhook upward into Ryan's left armpit, I block his left knee using my right hand.

4 Continuing to swim my left underhook upward, I step my left foot forward. Notice how I am avoiding Ryan's legs by walking in front of them.

5 I continue to drive into Ryan with my underhook and walk in front of his legs. Unable to step and regain his balance due to my right knee block, he begins collapsing to his back.

6 As Ryan collapses to his back, I drop down on top of him and establish the mount position.

Anderson Silva

Double-Leg Takedown off Cage

When you pin your opponent up against the fence, he loses his ability to defend against your double-leg takedown by sprawling, which is a serious advantage. However, the fence also limits your mobility. To get the takedown in this scenario, instead of driving your opponent straight back, you want to drop low, obtain control of his legs to limit his mobility, and then drive him laterally using your head. Unable to maintain his balance by stepping due to your leg control, he has no choice but to fall to the mat. If you look at the photos in the sequence below, you'll notice that throughout the duration of the move my opponent maintains an underhook, and it is possible for him to use his underhook to thwart my takedown attempt by keeping my body upright. To avoid this situation, you want to make a quick transition to his legs.

I have my opponent pinned against the cage. I have a left underhook, and he has a left underhook.

I quickly drop my level and place my left knee on the mat. At the same time, I hook my left arm around the back of my opponent's right leg and my right arm around the back of his left leg.

Pulling my opponent's right leg into me using my left arm, I rotate my upper body in a counterclockwise direction and drive my head into his left side. Unable to step his left foot to the outside of his body, he loses his balance and begins falling toward the mat.

Continuing to rotate and drive my head into my opponent's side, he collapses to the mat. Notice how I hug his legs tightly together to limit his ability to escape back to his feet.

As I drive my shoulders into my opponent's body to pin him to the mat, I begin walking around his legs in a counterclockwise direction.

I circle around to my opponent's left side. To secure side control, I release control of his legs and drive my knees into his body.

Randy Couture

High Crotch

When you rush forward and pin your opponent up against the fence, you'll usually end up in the over-under position. Although in the center of the cage the over-under position is neutral, your opponent is now backed up against the chain link, limiting his mobility. Sometimes this slight advantage allows you to drive forward and execute a double-leg takedown. If your opponent blocks the double-leg by holding your body up using his underhook, a good option is to abandon the double-leg, wrap your arms around just one of your opponent's legs, and secure the high-single position. Once you've established the position, walk your hips into your opponent, get your head up, and raise his center of gravity. You don't need to lift his feet off the mat, but this tends to happen when done with proper technique. With your opponent's center of gravity raised, pivot away from the fence to take away your opponent's backstop, causing him to fall naturally to the mat. It's a pretty basic technique—all you're doing is lifting your opponent up, and then stepping out to create a hole for him to fall into. Once your opponent hits the mat, he will have the fence against his back or side, which hinders his mobility and allows you to remain offensive.

With Ryan pinned against the cage, I'm attempting a double-leg takedown, but he is preventing me from dropping my elevation by holding my body upright using his left underhook.

Instead of fighting Ryan for the double-leg, I release my grip on his left leg, move my right arm between his legs, and then clasp my hands together on the inside of his right leg.

I step my left foot to the outside of Ryan's right foot, step my right foot between his legs, increase my elevation, and drive my hips into his body.

With my hands clasped firmly together, I continue to increase my elevation and pull Ryan off the mat. As I rotate my body in a counterclockwise direction, his body immediately begins to fall sideways.

I drop Ryan to his back.

To secure the side control position, I bend at the knees, drive my hips into Ryan's body, and posture up. From here, I will immediately begin a ground-and-pound assault.

Randy Couture

Guillotine Choke Defense (Running the Pipe)

When you pin your opponent up against the fence and are working for a takedown, a lot of the time it will require you to drop into a low stance. Occasionally your opponent will attempt to take advantage of your lowered elevation by wrapping up your head and arm and applying a guillotine choke. Instead of engaging in a hand fight to break his lock on your head, you scoop up his lead leg to establish the high-single position and then drive his body toward his missing leg. Just as with a table that is missing one of its legs, your opponent loses his balance and collapses as his weight shifts to that side of his body. The downside to this technique is that it doesn't work on all opponents. If your opponent has exceptional balance, he's going to hop on one leg and move around the corner as you're running pipe. In such a scenario, you should either move on to another takedown or begin defending against the choke.

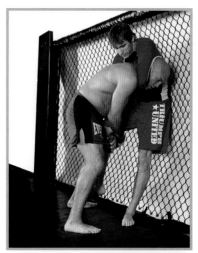

As I pin Ryan up against the cage, he wraps up my head and left arm and applies a guillotine choke.

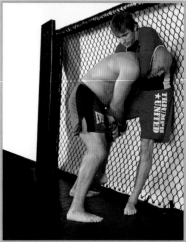

Before Ryan can tighten his grip and apply the choke, I pull his right leg up to my chest. Notice how his leg is positioned between my legs.

I slide my left foot across the mat in a counterclockwise direction. At the same time, I drive into Ryan's left side using my head. As his body turns toward his missing leg, he loses balance and begins falling toward his back.

As I continue to rotate into Ryan, he collapses to the mat and his lock on my head slips away.

As Ryan lands on his back, I maintain control of his right leg to prevent him from scrambling.

I lower my elevation by bending at the knees and drive my hips into Ryan's right leg. From this postured position, I will immediately begin a ground-and-pound assault.

Anderson Silva

Kimura Attack off Cage

In this scenario my opponent has me pressed against the cage and he is working for a high-single takedown. With my back pinned against the chain link, my defensive options are minimal. I am unable to move my hips backward due to the blockade behind me, I'm unable to circle my hips around his body due to his control, and I'm unable to force his head to the outside of my body because his elevation is too high. However, I still have one good option available—attacking his rear arm up with a kimura lock and then applying upward and outward pressure. The goal is not to lock in the kimura submission, but rather get my opponent to turn his body toward the fence to relieve the pressure being applied to his shoulder. As he turns, I turn with him. When his back is turned toward the cage, I slam my body into him and pin him up against the chain link. Once accomplished, I have reversed our positioning, giving me a couple of options. I can keep the kimura grip, roll my opponent to the mat, and attempt to finish the shoulder lock or I can release my hold and begin working my other cage tactics.

I'm pinned against the fence. My opponent has a deep left underhook and he has positioned his left leg deep between my legs. I must escape quickly.

Shifting my weight onto my left leg, I bend toward my left side and shoot my right arm over my opponent's head.

I reach my right arm around the outside of my opponent's right arm.

I hook my right arm around my opponent's upper right arm and then grab my left wrist with my right hand.

Using my kimura grip, I crank my opponent's arm upward and in a clockwise direction, putting a tremendous amount of stress on his shoulder.

As my opponent turns toward the cage to relieve the pressure from his shoulder, I turn with him.

As my opponent turns into the fence, I keep my kimura grip locked tight and drive my body into his body.

Anderson Silva

Reversal off Cage to Muay Thai Clinch

In this scenario, my opponent has my back pinned flat against the cage. With a dominant right underhook and his lead leg positioned deep between my legs, he has the very real option of clasping his hands together between my legs, lifting me off the mat, and dumping me to my back. To prevent him from utilizing this option, I quickly secure control of his rear wrist to prevent him from clasping his hands together. Next, I step my lead leg to the inside of his lead leg to eliminate his leverage to pick me up off the mat. Once accomplished, I can now switch from defense to offense. I do this by driving my lead knee into my opponent's hips to force his body away from me. This creates an ample amount of space between our bodies, allowing me to slide my lead elbow in front of his shoulder and secure a collar tie. With more freedom of movement, I then circle around my opponent, release control of his rear arm, and secure a second collar tie, giving me the Muay Thai clinch. Without delay, I pull my opponent's head down and begin landing brutal knee strikes to his midsection. The most important part of this technique is controlling both of your opponent's arms as you drive his body away from you using your lead knee. If you look at the photos below, you'll notice that as I perform this action I'm controlling my opponent's far arm by gripping his wrist and his near arm with a Whizzer. If you use this technique against a wrestler and fail to control both of his arms, the instant you drive his body away from you using your knee, he will most likely drop his elevation, wrap his arms around your lead leg, and secure the single-leg position.

I'm pinned against the fence. My opponent has established a left underhook and stepped his right leg deep between my legs. Immediately I wrap my left arm over his right arm, establishing a tight whizzer.

Keeping my whizzer tight, I step my left foot around to the front of my opponent's right foot.

I take an outward step with my right foot, and then drive my left knee into my opponent's right thigh to create separation between us.

Continuing to drive my left knee into my opponent's right thigh, I pull my upper body away from him, release my whizzer, and wrap my left hand around the back of his neck.

I secure a left collar tie by positioning my left elbow in front of my opponent's right shoulder. This allows me to maintain space between our bodies. Next, I pull my left knee away from his right thigh.

I rotate my body in a counterclockwise direction, release my right grip on my opponent's left wrist, cup my right hand over my left hand, and position my right elbow in front of his body.

Having secured the Muay Thai clinch, I pull my opponent's head down and deliver a straight right knee to his sternum.

Anderson Silva

Backdoor Slide-By Reversal off Cage

In this scenario my opponent has my back pinned against the cage just as in the last, but now I have a deep underhook with my right arm. Before he has a chance to secure an underhook of his own, I grab his free wrist and force it away from my body. At the same time, I swim my underhook upward into his arm, creating space between us. This allows me to reach my underhook arm around his back and secure a second grip on his free wrist. Once accomplished, I have prevented my opponent from being able to turn into me. Now I am able to release my initial grip on his wrist, slide out from underneath my opponent's overhook, and take his back. The most important part of this technique is securing control of your opponent's free wrist with your underhook arm. If you fail to do this, as you slide out the back door your opponent can simply turn into you and keep your back pinned to the fence.

I'm pinned against the cage. I have established a right underhook.

As I drop my elevation by sliding my back down the cage, I force my opponent's right arm away from my body using my left hand. At the same time, I swim my right arm upward into my opponent's left arm, creating space between our bodies.

I reach my right arm around my opponent's back and grip his right forearm.

Keeping my right grip tight, I release my left grip on my opponent's wrist and begin sliding my body out from underneath his left arm. Due to my control, he is unable to turn back into me and stop my transition.

I bend forward at the waist, circle around behind my opponent, and continue to pull my body out from underneath his left arm.

I circle toward my opponent's back.

Freeing my body out from underneath my opponent's left arm, I circle around behind him and take his back. From here, I have the option of securing back control or pushing my opponent away and striking. Here I chose the latter.

Anderson Silva

Single-Leg to Far Ankle Pick

In the previous sequence I demonstrated how to circle around behind your opponent when your back is pressed up against the cage and you have a deep underhook. It's an excellent option to have in your arsenal, but if your opponent is familiar with the clinch, chances are he will drive down into your body with his overhook, severing the space you need to circle out from underneath his arm and take his back. Rather than fight your opponent's downward pressure, you move with it in this technique by sliding your back down the fence and dropping your level. Your opponent's arm will most likely follow you, still preventing you from taking his back, but with your hips now lower than his hips, you are in a good position to attack with the ankle pick takedown demonstrated below.

I'm pinned against the fence. However, I've managed to secure a right underhook.

With my opponent applying downward pressure with his left whizzer, I am unable to circle around behind his back. Instead, I slide my back down the fence and drop my left knee toward the mat. At the same time, I reach my right arm around his body and force his right arm away from me using my left hand.

I wrap my right arm around my opponent's back and grab his right forearm. At the same time, I circle toward his back and hook my left leg around his left leg.

Maintaining a tight grip on my opponent's right arm, I release my left grip on his wrist and grab his right instep with my left hand. Next, I drive into his body.

I continue to drive into my opponent. With my left leg hooked around his left leg, he is unable to step forward with his left foot. And with my left hand hooked around his right instep, he is unable to step with his right foot. As a result, he begins falling toward the mat.

As my opponent lands on his right side, I come down on top of him and close off all space to prevent him from scrambling to his feet or a more dominant position.

Outside Trip

This technique comes into play in the same scenario as the last—your back is pinned up against the cage, you have an underhook, but your opponent prevents you from circling around to his back by applying downward pressure with his overhook. Just as in the previous technique, you go with your opponent's downward pressure by sliding your back down the cage and dropping your level. However, instead of driving into your opponent and executing the ankle pick, you circle in a clockwise direction to face your opponent, hook a leg behind his leg, and drive him down to his back. Neither the outside trip nor the ankle pick is superior. As a matter of fact, they work extremely well when combined. If your opponent defends the ankle pick, you have an easy transition to the outside trip. And if your opponent defends against the outside trip, you have an easy transition to the ankle pick.

I've got my back pressed up against the fence, but I've managed to secure a double underhook body lock.

I rotate my upper body in a counterclockwise direction to create space and force my opponent to take an outward step with his right foot.

As my opponent plants his right foot to the outside of his body, I shift my weight onto my right leg, drop my elevation, and position my head in font of my opponent's chest.

I rotate in a clockwise direction and position my body in front of my opponent. At the same time, I hook my right leg around the outside of his left leg and begin driving him backward.

Due to my right leg hook, my opponent is unable to step back to maintain his balance. As a result, he falls toward his back as I continue to drive into him.

As my opponent lands on his back, I come down on top of him and close off all space to prevent him from scrambling.

Anderson Silva

Knee Blast - Block Reversal into Cage

In this scenario I'm in the over-under clinch with my back pinned against the fence. My opponent has stepped his lead leg deep between my legs, putting me in a very dangerous position. At any moment he can drop his elevation, secure control of my hips, and attack with a takedown. To prevent him from accomplishing this goal, I am going to use my positioning in the over-under clinch to execute a knee blast to reverse my opponent into the cage. The goal of this technique is to drive upward with your underhook, forcing your opponent to the side. However, right before you execute the upward lift with your underhook, you reach down with your overhook arm and block your opponent's knee with your hand. This prevents him from stepping outward and maintaining his balance as you drive into him with your underhook, causing him to fall over your arm. When this technique is used in the center of the cage or in wrestling matches, your opponent usually trips over your arm and lands on his back, but because you're using it while pressed up against the cage, he falls back into the cage instead. To make the most of the situation, drive into his body to reverse your positioning. Due to the swimming motion you made with your underhook, the majority of the time your opponent will get pinned in a very awkward position. If his arm is pinned over his head, it allows you to move your underhook to the inside of his overhook and establish a collar tie, giving you the dirty boxing clinch.

I'm pressed up against the cage in the over-under clinch.

Rotating in a clockwise direction, I block my opponent's left knee with my right hand. At the same time, I drive my left underhook upward into his right arm.

Keeping my opponent's left knee blocked, I pivot on my right foot, slide my left foot in a clockwise direction across the mat, and turn his back toward the cage using my left underhook.

I drive my opponent's back into the cage using my left underhook and then immediately close off all space between our bodies.

I turn my left shoulder into my opponent's body to pin him to the fence and create space on our right side. At the same time, I begin the process of eliminating his underhook by placing my right hand on his left biceps.

I eliminate my opponent's left underhook by pinning his arm to the fence using my right hand.

I slide my left arm out from underneath my opponent's right arm, hook my hand around the back of his neck, and then position my left elbow in front of his chest. This gives me a collar tie.

Forcing my opponent's head down and toward his left side using my collar tie, I pull my right arm back and prepare to throw elbows to his unprotected face.

Anderson Silva

Duck-Under to Rear Naked Choke

In this sequence my opponent has pressed my back up against the fence, but I have managed to secure a double underhook body lock. Although I'm in a better position than in previous sequences due to my dominant clinch, my offensive options are limited with my back pinned against the chain link. To make my escape, I execute a move called the duck-under, which is similar to the slide-by shown earlier. With both techniques the goal is to move underneath your opponent's arm and circle around his torso until you reach his back. However, it is important to note that the technique shown below is only possible because my opponent makes the mistake of not clamping down on my underhooks with tight overhooks, giving me space to work. It makes for an easy transition to his back. Although you should never count on your opponent making this mistake in a fight, you need to be ready to capitalize on it when he does. If you look at the photos below, you'll notice that once I take my opponent's back I don't simply disengage. Instead, I secure back control, drop straight down to my butt, and then kick my shins into the back of my opponent's legs to destroy his balance and make sure he comes with me. Next, I use one arm to hinder his choke defenses while I wrap the opposite arm around his neck. Once accomplished, I lock in a rear naked choke, squeeze, and force my opponent to tap.

I'm pressed against the fence, but I have managed to secure a double underhook body lock.

My opponent is not applying much downward pressure with his overhook, so I begin circling toward his back by bending my body toward my left side and dropping my elevation.

I step my right leg around behind my opponent's back and begin pulling my head out from underneath his left arm.

I pull my head all the way out from underneath my opponent's left arm, and circle around to back control.

Once I reach my opponent's back, I immediately drop my elevation by bending my knees.

I sit my butt straight down to the mat and kick my shins into the back of my opponent's legs to destroy his balance and pull him with me.

As I roll to my back, I use my legs to elevate my opponent's legs off the mat.

As I rock my weight forward, my opponent sits up in an attempt to escape my control.

I sit up into my opponent and wrap my left arm over his left shoulder. Notice how my legs are still hooked underneath his legs to prevent him from scrambling.

I grab my opponent's right arm using my left hand. This hinders him from using his arms to defend against the choke. At the same time, I wrap my right arm around his neck.

I release control of my opponent's right arm, grab my left biceps with my right hand, and then begin moving my left hand toward the back of his head.

I place my left hand on the back of my opponent's head, roll to my right side, hook my legs over his legs, and then finish the choke by squeezing my arms tight.

INSTRUCTIONAL BOOKS

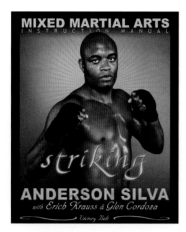

***MIXED MARTIAL ARTS
INSTRUCTION MANUAL***

ANDERSON SILVA

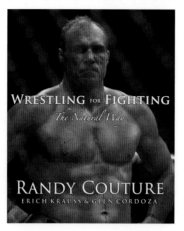

WRESTLING FOR FIGHTING

RANDY COUTURE

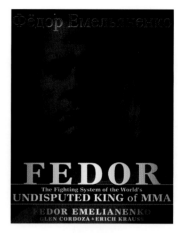

FEDOR

FEDOR
EMELIANENKO

MASTERING THE RUBBER GUARD

EDDIE BRAVO

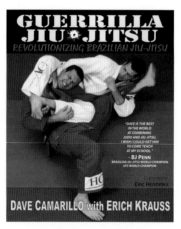

GUERRILLA JIU-JITSU

DAVE CAMARILLO

JUDO FOR MIXED MARTIAL ARTS

KARO PARISYAN

THE X-GUARD

MARCELO GARCIA

MASTERING THE TWISTER

EDDIE BRAVO

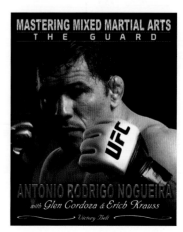

MASTERING MIXED MARTIAL ARTS

ANTONIO RODRIGO
NOGUEIRA

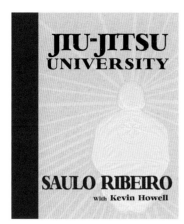

JIU-JITSU UNIVERSITY
SAULO RIBEIRO

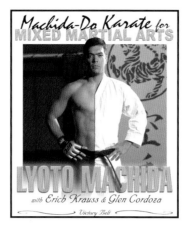

MACHIDA-DO KARATE FOR MIXED MARTIAL ARTS
LYOTO MACHIDA

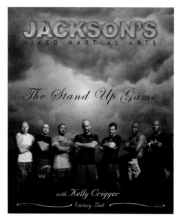

JACKSON'S MIXED MARTIAL ARTS: THE STAND UP GAME
GREG JACKSON

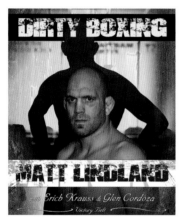

DIRTY BOXING
MATT LINDLAND

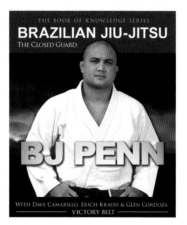

BRAZILIAN JIU-JITSU: THE CLOSED GUARD
BJ PENN

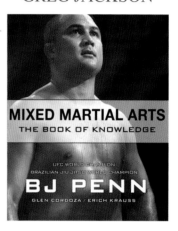

DVDs

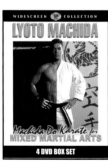

MACHIDA-DO KARATE FOR MIXED MARTIAL ARTS
LYOTO MACHIDA

GUARD FOR MMA
ANTONIO RODRIGO NOGUEIRA

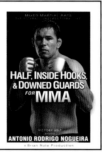

HALF, INSIDE HOOKS, & DOWNED GUARD FOR MMA
ANTONIO RODRIGO NOGUEIRA

PASSING FOR MMA
ANTONIO RODRIGO NOGUEIRA

MASTERING THE RUBBER GUARD (DVD)
EDDIE BRAVO

BOXING FOR MMA
ANDERSON SILVA

MUAY THAI STRIKING FOR MMA
ANDERSON SILVA

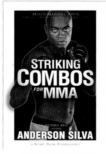

STRIKING COMBOS FOR MMA
ANDERSON SILVA

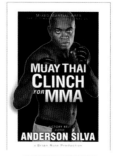

MUAY THAI CLINCH FOR MMA
ANDERSON SILVA

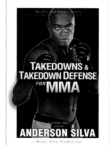

TAKEDOWNS & TAKEDOWN DEFENSE FOR MMA
ANDERSON SILVA

About the Author

Erich Krauss is the *New York Times Bestselling* author of Forrest Griffin's *Got Fight: The Fifty Zen Principles of Hand-to-Face Combat*, and he has written more than twenty five books. He is also a professional Muay Thai kickboxer who has lived and fought in Thailand. He lives in Las Vegas, Nevada.